This book is published to accompany the television series entitled *Strictly Come Dancing*, first broadcast on BBC1 in 2013.

Executive Producer: Louise Rainbow
Creative Consultant: Andrea Hamilton
Series Producer: Jayne Stanger

With thanks to Kim Winston, Claire Bridgland, Mike Briffith, Natalie Alvarado and Jason Gilkison.

1 3 5 7 9 10 8 6 4 2

Published in 2013 by BBC Books, an imprint of Ebury Publishing. A Random House Group Company.

Strictly Come Dancing logo ™ & © BBC 2013, BBC logo ™ & © BBC 1996.
Devised by the BBC and Licensed by BBC Worldwide Limited.
Text by Alison Maloney
Introductions by Sir Bruce Forsyth and Tess Daly
Copyright © Woodlands Books Ltd 2013

The Random House Group Limited Reg. No. 954009

Addresses for companies within the Random House Group can be found at www.randomhouse.co.uk

A CIP catalogue record for this book is available from the British Library.

ISBN: 978 1 84990 667 8

Commissioning editor: Lorna Russell
Project editors: Kate Fox and Lizzy Gaisford
Design: Karin Fremer

Printed and bound in Germany by Mohn Media GmbH

To buy books by your favourite authors and register for offers visit www.randomhouse.co.uk

Strictly Come Dancing

The Official 2014 Annual

Alison Maloney

BOOKS

CONTENTS

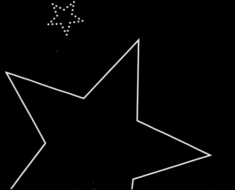

MEET THIS YEAR'S STARS

BRUCE FORSYTH

It's early days but this year's *Strictly* looks like it's shaping up to be a good one. It takes a few weeks before we really see what the show is all about. But we've got some great characters in the line-up and the celebrity group dance at the launch show was the best routine yet.

Sophie Ellis-Bextor and Brendan Cole look like a promising couple and she was very pleased to get Brendan. Natalie Gumede is partnering Artem, who's a very hard taskmaster but knows what he's looking for. They are definitely a couple to watch.

I was thrilled that Anton Du Beke got Fiona Fullerton because he's had a bit of bad luck over the years, and he's taken it all in good part. Fiona will be a lovely partner. She'll not only be fun, and eternally elegant, but I think she'll also put in some good dances. I haven't seen her since we made a Christmas special with Ronnie Corbett, which, Fiona kindly reminded me, was 25 years ago!

As a keen golfer, Tony Jacklin is a hero of mine. We have known each other a lifetime and played quite a few rounds in our time. Once, when I was filming a series in Leeds, I kept a whole studio waiting so I could watch him win the British Open. I sent a message down to the director saying, 'I've got to wait until Tony sinks the last putt, and then I'll work until midnight if I have to.' He'd just won the US Open and had come back home to take the British Open, which was a rare feat.

Our first fashion designer, Julien Macdonald, could be giving the wardrobe department a run for their money, but he'll be fun. Deborah Meaden is full of life and is going into it whole-heartedly. It will make a change for her to get up and do something after sitting in the *Dragons' Den* chair for so long.

We have plenty of young glamour, with the likes of Abbey Clancy and Rachel Riley and, as usual, a good range of ages. Everyone loves to see an older person having a go, too – which is why Pamela Stephenson was great, and why Ann Widdecombe was so popular. She didn't always know what she was doing, but she gave it her best shot.

Last year was a fantastic series. Out of the last four couples, or even six, any one of them would have been worthy winners so it was terribly close, which made it interesting. From a dancing point of view, the last few weeks couldn't have been better.

Strictly is now celebrating ten years, and here I still am for the eleventh series! It will be lovely working with Tess again and I can't wait to get started. This year, having satisfied the frustrated performer in me with shows at Glastonbury and the Albert Hall, I am enjoying *Strictly* more than ever and having even more fun.

I don't have a crystal ball – just a glitterball – but I think we are in for a wonderful series.

TESS DALY

Every year at *Strictly* we say, 'This is our biggest series yet' and, this year, it is genuinely true. We've got a bigger cast of celebrities, with 15 couples, and the show runs for a week longer. We also have five hot, new dancers, including Aljaž, who proved a huge hit with the ladies at the launch show!

Natalie Gumede is looking good from the off and she and Artem are the couple to watch. He is a hard taskmaster and there's no second best as far as Artem is concerned. Abbey Clancy shows a lot of potential, and Ashley Taylor Dawson, inspired by our reigning champ Louis Smith, has been doing gymnastics so that he can pull out all the stops and do a few tricks.

Personality is one thing we are not short of in this line-up. I can't wait to see Vanessa Feltz make mincemeat of Craig. He's actually quite nervous for the first time because I think he may have met his match. Our *Hairy Biker* Dave Myers is going to be entertaining, without a doubt. He's such a character and you can't help but love him.

Fashion designer Julien Macdonald is the first celebrity we've had on the show who's said, 'Give me more sequins!' He has a theory that the more sequins he wears, the less people will look at his feet.

We have lots of glamour – gorgeous ladies and some pretty hot guys. Ben Cohen seems quite fond of stripping off his clothes and posing on magazine covers, so he won't be shy when it comes to ripping off his shirt for the paso doble. He could be a grower, dancing wise. The sportsmen can often be slow burners because they are not used to the performance side of it, but once they find their dancing feet – like Mark Ramprakash and Darren Gough – they can go all the way.

Fiona Fullerton is a huge *Strictly* fan and every Saturday night the whole family watch the show together. Now she's on it and over the moon. She also has a ten-year crush on Len Goodman – she's absolutely besotted.

If I were to give the contestants any advice, I'd say, 'Forget the rest of your lives because from now on *Strictly* is your life. If you don't fully engage with this, you're not going to get anywhere.' There's no such thing as a day off once the competition starts hotting up. Susanna and Vanessa are both on breakfast shows, so they've got to do a full day's work before training, which will be tough. You need stamina on this show, that's for sure.

This is the tenth year of *Strictly*, and it's still the most glamorous show on TV. It has entered the nation's consciousness and there's genuine affection for it. As far as I'm concerned, every new series brings excitement and I can't wait to start. So when Saturday night rolls around, get in the party mood, get the popcorn out and … keeeeeep dancing!

WHAT'S NEW?

After ten happy years in Television Centre, *Strictly* is waltzing off to a new home at the BBC's Elstree Studios. Managing the move is the new executive producer, Louise Rainbow, who reveals the show will be bigger and better.

'*W*e are going to make much more of a feature of our orchestra,' she explains. 'In previous years Dave Arch and his musicians have been down a dark hole at the back of the stage, but the new area is wider, with a bandstand, and tiers to show off the musicians, so it definitely has more of a big-band feel.

'The dance floor is slightly bigger, so there is plenty of room for the group performances, and the audience numbers will go from around 600 to more than 700, so more people can be part of the show.'

Another addition is an extra couple – so there will be 15 celebrities instead of the usual 14 – and there will be five new professionals on the dance floor, following the departure of Vincent, Flavia and Erin.

'Having new dancers in the mix will add a little extra frisson,' says Louise. 'Those dancers who aren't competing in the series will still be part of the *Strictly* family. For instance, we are hoping that Flavia and Vincent will be able to come back to perform in our Xmas special.'

The *Strictly Come Dancing* logo is getting a glitzy makeover, and the whole feel of the show is going back to old-school glamour. 'It will all look very contemporary but celebrate a very classic, chic style – glossy, high end and aspirational.'

But Louise, who has produced many BBC shows including *Let's Dance for Comic Relief,* says viewers won't see any dramatic overhauls.

Countdown to the première: Rachel Riley gets the Hollywood look for the big night.

Casualty star Patrick Robinson goes back to 'old school glamour' for the big opening night.

Another innovation for series 11 is the appointment of a head of choreography in Jason Gilkison. The former dancer and his partner Peta Roby were undefeated Australian Latin champions from 1981 to 1997, and he has since worked as choreographer on *Dancing with the Stars* in the US, *Burn the Floor* and contributed to two series of *Strictly*.

'Normally I come in just for a couple of weeks, and last year I did Wembley,' he explains. 'So it's going to be good to follow something right the way through, and it's exciting because *Strictly* has never had this before.'

As well as crafting a few group numbers, Jason will be overseeing all the dances. 'I'm there as a sounding board for the pros when they're working out their celeb routines,' he says. 'If they're at a dead end they can come to me and work through some ideas, but they're still doing their own choreography.'

Through his past work, Jason knows all the pro dancers well, and even taught some when they were children – which helps a lot during training.

'I worked with Brendan 15 years ago, and I remember James as a young kid in the dance studio. They don't pull any nonsense in front of me because I've known them for too long. They're a good bunch to work with and they really work as a team. It's such a nice environment.'

'We don't want to lose the atmosphere, the intensity and the intimacy that you have on *Strictly*. Viewers have always felt like they were close to the action and we're not going to lose that. The judges will be in the same place, the arches are still there and Tess still has her balcony, so we're not making any overly radical changes.

Louise says she was 'over the moon' to be asked to take over the show. 'I wake up every morning excited to go to work. It's a very precious gift so you nurture it and try and make it even better.

'Last year was an amazing year and that's opened up a few doors for us. I'm excited about the calibre of celebrity we have and about their enthusiasm for the show. In my opinion, we have some potential dancing talent in this year's line-up.'

New head of choreography Jason Gilkison worked wonders at last year's Wembley show.

LOUIS SMITH

After bagging a silver and bronze at the London 2012 Olympics, Louis Smith was aiming to impress as soon as he hit the dance floor. His week 1 cha-cha-cha had Bruno declaring him a 'snake-hipped wonder' and, combined with his high-scoring Viennese waltz, left him looking like one to watch.

But as an Olympic gymnast, he is used to highs and lows – and it wasn't all plaudits and podiums for the 26 year old. Despite an open shirt to reveal his impressive pecs, his week 5 samba left Darcey feeling 'Disappointed' as she felt it 'was a bit safe'. The following week a romantic waltz was dubbed 'very pedestrian' by Craig, who gave a low score of 6, and his Wembley week American smooth left the judges underwhelmed, with Bruno telling him, 'It wasn't bad but you can do better.'

Louis and Flavia take the prize after a thrilling final.

Wembley was my worst moment, because that was the worst performance of the series for me,' says Louis. 'The show, the production, the crowd were unbelievable ... but the dance wasn't very good.'

After Len declared his next dance, the paso doble, had 'no fire', it was literally time to act. Flavia called in a drama coach to teach Louis some tips, and things began to look up. Their week 9 Charleston blew the judges away.

The Charleston was my breakthrough after the acting lessons,' he recalls. 'They worked. I gave a lot of performance, I really put a lot into it, and it was a turning point for me in the competition.'

Delighted fans got a second dose of the dance – which saw Louis dressed as a doctor to Flavia's palpitating patient – when the couple chose it for the last dance of the final, and Bruno declared it was 'just what the doctor ordered.' And after a topless, barefoot show dance, it got the public pulses racing enough to bag him the glitterball.

Above: 'No fire': Len criticised the pair's paso for lack of drama.
Opposite: Flipping amazing! Louis puts his gymnastic skills into the Charleston.

Above: Mat-adorable! Louis gets bullish in the paso doble, which failed to impress judges.
Opposite: Louis's final dance opened with a dramatic and daring balancing act.

'Picking up the trophy felt good,' Louis says. 'I was a bit nervous, a bit excited, a bit upset that it was all coming to an end. But I had a brilliant time; I loved every minute of it – and I'd do it all again and again.'

The win came at the end of an incredible year for the athlete, who picked up the silver medal for the men's pommel horse at the London Olympics and a bronze in the artistic team event.

'Everything was pretty full on all year, but it was amazing,' he says. 'Winning *Strictly* is a different sense of achievement. My Olympic medals will be with me for the rest of my life, whatever happens. Money comes and goes but I'll always have those. But the glitterball – wow! Little old me from Peterborough going into a show like that and actually winning is remarkable. I still can't get over it.'

As a competing athlete, what Louis initially lacked in acting skills, he more than made up for in fitness. But even he found the training tough. 'I thought I would be more used to the training than anyone else, but it's very different from what I'm used to,' he admits.

'But the advantage I have is that I know my body quite well; so I know what I need to do to get the job done. There is no point in me spending 12 hours in a dance studio, because it will just end up going downhill. So I do a steady six hours a day, every day.'

Flavia took his intense approach on board and got her reward when she finally got her hands on the coveted trophy.

'Flavia really understood me quite early on, which made both our lives a lot easier,' reveals Louis. 'I'm not the easiest person to work with, but I do work if you get me in the right frame of mind, in the right mood, which she did very well. She was brilliant, and one of the loveliest people I've ever met.'

With Olympic glory and the *Strictly* crown behind him the only question for Louis is how he will top 2012. 'I don't know if I can,' he laughs. 'And I don't know if I want to. It was fantastic. I think if I ever have a better year it will be when I have a child with my wife. But as I haven't got a wife, or even a girlfriend yet, that might take a while!'

Louis's advice to the class of 2013

'Be patient with it. Embrace it. Enjoy it. Don't take it too seriously. Don't get too caught up in it. Have fun with your partner. Work your socks off but enjoy it while you're doing it because it's very short and it's very sad when it's over.'

BRUNO

Another high-flying series saw Bruno Tonioni parachuted into Wembley alongside fellow judge Craig. But the jet-setting judge is hoping that's one landing he'll never have to repeat.

'I'm not doing that again!' he insists. 'I don't like heights anyway so it was dreadful. You do these things once, but never again. No more flying for me – I'll leave that to Ann Widdecombe.'

There were more enjoyable moments and a few giggles for the flamboyant Italian. 'My favourite moment was when I nearly died of laughter with Lisa Riley, after I uttered a naughty word,' he says. 'We just cracked and couldn't stop. There was a big hoo-ha and everyone was falling over. It was funny!'

Here's Bruno's version of events for series 10.

Was Louis Smith a worthy winner?
The body is the evidence. But Louis had to work for it, it wasn't a given. He always had a natural rhythm but at the beginning he couldn't quite emote and express. It all changed on Halloween night when he found his sexy zombie, and he really came up with the goods when he did his final freestyle dance.

Did you think he would win?
It was very close. Kimberley looked amazing, but she was a little weak to start with though when she found her strength she was dazzling! Denise was technically one of the best dancers we've ever had. I had no idea which way it would go, and the final was incredible.

Louis and Flavia bag their first 9s for a spooktastic Halloween tango

Biggest surprise?

Lisa Riley for entertainment value and energy. She made the most of what she had and was so entertaining to watch. She gave amazing performances and we were very surprised – in a good way. She totally embraced the show. Adorable.

Who do you wish had stayed longer?

Victoria Pendleton seemed an ideal competitor, having done so well at the Olympics, but she didn't quite click. Still looked beautiful on the floor, though, and tried her best which is what the show is all about. Jerry Hall, as I said, was great when she was standing still.

Who improved the most?

Nicky Byrne started very rough and I thought he did very well. He worked extremely hard and he wasn't one of the best dancers, but he improved an awful lot. So did Louis, because his scores at the beginning weren't that high.

Victoria and Brendan are in a New York state of mind for their week 6 Quickstep.

Outstanding moments from series 10?

Denise did an incredible jive, then there was the Egyptian number, the Charleston. That was just superb. Louis's freestyle was outstanding too.

How was it having Darcey on the panel?

I loved it. I knew her before and she's so easy to get on with. She fitted in perfectly and all the feedback from the public was positive. It was a match made in heaven. My only wish is that she were next to me, to give me a break from Len!

Nicky Byrne ups his game with an impressive week 8 Charleston.

17

Sophie ELLIS-BEXTOR

The stunning singer will be hoping she's not 'Murder on the Dance Floor' as she takes to the *Strictly* stage. But her fellow celebs may have more to worry about, particularly if they watch the video for the hit, which sees her picking off contestants in a dance competition one by one.

'If you follow the video through to the end,' she laughs, 'I actually win the competition by using some devious methods, so the others better watch out!'

The Hounslow-born songstress, daughter of former *Blue Peter* presenter Janet Ellis, burst on to the pop scene when she collaborated with Spiller on the dance-track hit 'Groovejet (If This Ain't Love)'. Going straight in at number one, and beating Victoria Beckham's first solo outing to the top spot, the track won numerous Best Single awards and went platinum. Sophie followed with a solo album and two smash singles, 'Take Me Home' and 'Murder on the Dance Floor'. She is also a successful DJ and model, and is now a mum to three boys. But it was her girlfriends who persuaded her to swap dance music for dance floor.

'When I mentioned the possibility of doing it, their whole body language changed and they went, "Oh my God! *Strictly*!" They went off on one,' she reveals. 'They told me, "If you're doing that we'd be as excited as if you were having another baby!"

'I just thought, I can't say no because my girlfriends want to be doing this, so if you're asked to do it, you've got to do it. It's once in a lifetime.'

The 34 year old is currently trying to resist the lure of the spray tan. 'I've never had one in my life,' she says. 'I don't tan in the sun. I've got this one shade. But I think if I try it and I like it, then I'm doomed, because I'll have to keep it up for ever!

'I'm shunning it so far. I just know it's going to happen. If it does, I'll go for a properly dark colour. It's got to be noticeable!'

Partnered with fiery professional Brendan Cole, the petite brunette says she's prepared to be put through her paces in training.

'I don't know what I'm doing so it's to be expected,' she reasons. 'Bring it on!'

Brendan COLE

The bad boy of *Strictly* danced the very first dance of series 1, with Natasha Kaplinsky, and was the first to lift the glittering prize. Ten years on, he and Anton are the only original professionals left. So what does he think makes the show such a success?

'Anton and me, obviously!' he jokes. But he adds, 'There is a magic about *Strictly*. We're the only people in the world doing this sort of show and it's a phenomenal bubble to be in. You feel so special. It's hard work but when you put the glad rags on, when you're walking out, when Bruce and Tess come down the stairs, it's magical.'

The New Zealander comes from a family of dancers and, at his mum's insistence, started classes in Christchurch at six. Although he says he hated it, he had a natural flair and soon became the Juvenile, Junior and Youth Champion of New Zealand.

At 18, he moved to the UK where he met Camilla Dallerup, who became his dancing partner for eight years. They taught in Hong Kong before signing for *Strictly*.

Initially known for his fiery temper and illegal lifts, Brendan says he has mellowed over the last ten years.

'I've changed a lot,' he reveals. 'You learn what not to do. Everyone has their good and bad sides. Sometimes you want something that you can't achieve, and it doesn't work, so you waste all your time trying to force it. But you learn a lot as you go and get on board with what the whole thing is about, rather than worrying just about you.'

After a decade on the *Strictly* dance floor, Brendan admits he still gets excited as each new series approaches.

'When the show finishes in December, I am completely exhausted!' he says. 'It is gruellingly tough, but only physically. Emotionally, you miss it. When it comes around again you think, It's getting closer! and then it takes over your life again.'

CRAIG

Series 10 saw Craig Revel Horwood dressed up as the Tin Man, parachuting from the rafters of Wembley, dancing with Darcey and cackling like a maniac at the end of a 'Thriller' dance. But the honest Aussie says he loves showing his lighter side.

'I get asked to do the most ridiculous things,' he says. 'But I'm up for a laugh and I like to take the mickey out of myself so that people know I am not as serious as I appear on the judges' panel. For the show's opening I can be as silly as I want.'

On the dance floor, however, he was pleased that the comedy was kept to a minimum. 'This year there weren't any obvious comic turns. Richard Arnold, of course, was as camp as a row of tents and he was fun, but there wasn't a clown, an Ann Widdecombe or a John Sergeant, which was refreshing.'

Being Olympic year, Craig was thrilled to see two medal winners among the contestants, and thought it fitting that Louis struck gold in the final. 'I didn't expect Louis to win, but he was loved by everyone, and the entire UK was going mad for the Olympics, so it seems only right.'

Was Louis a worthy winner?

He wasn't entirely the judges' choice because there were better dancers, but he was the people's choice. The show is about what thrills the audience, particularly in the final when we don't have any say.

He was entertaining, good-looking, and he's probably been one of our best rumba boys ever because he has a nice straight leg and beautiful hip action. His dances were chosen wisely and choreographed beautifully by Flavia.

Louis's Olympic effort on the dance floor.

Richard Arnold camps it up for maximum effect.

Who was the biggest surprise?

Lisa Riley was a pleasant surprise, because I didn't expect her to be able to dance as well as she could and to be able to move around the dance floor so fluently. I hope she made a lot of people think, Wow, maybe I could dance. She was wonderful and she filled the entire space with energy, vivacity and personality.

Who improved the most?

For me, Nicky Byrne. He started badly and Westlife fans were hating me and sending me ghastly messages, but it wasn't my fault he couldn't dance! He worked really hard though, and it showed. For someone who was quite awkward, he ended up doing some very impressive dances.

How did Darcey do as the new judge?

The first couple of weeks must have been daunting – you've got 12 million people assessing you and hanging on your every word. It's nerve-racking but I think she did it brilliantly in the end. She really became herself and became a natural. It's not as easy as it looks!

Nicky Byrne went from 'awkward' to 'impressive' tango.

Who do you think was the best dancer?

Denise Van Outen, definitely. Kimberley was a close second and I loved Dani Harmer. The final was one of the most amazing we've ever had to judge. Denise, Kimberly and Dani were so close. You could pick holes in Louis but he won the hearts and minds of the nation.

Favourite dance of the series?

I really loved Denise's Egyptian Charleston, which was incredible. Her jive was equally spectacular. She really suited both those dances. I also loved Louis's tango/rumba fusion.

Patrick ROBINSON

The *Casualty* star is swapping his white coat for something a little more glittery for the dance floor – and he can't wait.

'I'm very good with the Lycra and the sparkly, sparkly,' Patrick laughs. 'It's all good as far as I'm concerned.'

As a busy soap star, Patrick is going to have to fit training around the day job – and that means partner Anya Garnis will be spending a lot of time in Wales.

'How much time I have is down to the producers,' he explains. '*Casualty* is shot in Cardiff, so it just depends how much they make me work. There may be a lot of dancing on the wards. It's a big studio and they shoot quite a few shows down there, including *Doctor Who* and *Wizards vs Aliens*, so there's plenty of space. I think I will be working and then go and do some training with Anya, then go back to work.'

The Londoner was classically trained at LAMDA (London Academy of Music and Dramatic Art) before joining the Royal Shakespeare Company, where he was the first-ever black actor to play Romeo in *Romeo and Juliet*.

In 1990, he landed the role of a charge nurse in the medical drama *Casualty*, leaving after six and a half years. In 2013, 17 years on, he made his return to the series as a doctor.

An avid Arsenal fan, his *Strictly* hero is fellow Gooner Mark Ramprakash. 'He was so fabulous,' says Patrick. 'I played football with him for the Arsenal ex-professional and celebrity team. One of the things about Mark is that he is lovely, and he was brilliant, so he is the hero to try and emulate.'

The soap star keeps himself fit and has been putting in a few extra classes in the run-up to the show. 'The only extra stuff I have done, other than my usual work-out and bike rides is some more stretching, flexibility exercises. I have done a little bit of yoga, but that's about it.'

On the subject of ballroom prowess, the 49-year-old heartthrob says his dancing feet don't work as well as they used to. 'When I was very young I would say my dancing skills were like a 7 or 8.5, not bad – I could try my hand at everything,' he recalls. 'Now you are looking at a 4 or 5, so if I get anything above a 6 I will be very chuffed.'

Anya GARNIS

Anya's arrival on the *Strictly* set means a special reunion for one established professional. Two-time finalist Pasha Kovalev was her dance partner for 12 years, after they met in their teens at a Russian dance school.

'Pasha and I danced together until a couple of years ago,' she explains. 'It's going to be wonderful to be reunited with him and he's been doing so well, so I'm very happy for him. Now we are coming back together, we'll see how we've grown, which is the most exciting part.'

Born in Latvia and raised in Siberia, Anya fell in love with dancing when a friend took her along to watch at the age of eight. 'I saw all the beautiful dresses and glamorous ladies, and that's when I decided to learn ballroom.'

At 13, she left home, with the blessing of her parents, to study at a school near Moscow, where she met Pasha. At 16, she became his dance partner and, a year later, they turned professional in order to move to the US, where they became finalists in the National Latin championship.

The couple's big break came when they auditioned for *So You Think You Can Dance*. 'We made it through the show and then other opportunities unfolded for us, which were amazing. We danced on Broadway for *Burn the Floor*, and then we travelled the world with them. Pasha left for London then, while Anya stayed in the US, doing film and TV work and a five-month stint in *Dancing with the Stars: Live in Las Vegas*, before signing up to *Strictly*, and she says she's 'super-ecstatic' about her new role.

Pasha isn't her only friend on the show. 'Janette is like my sister and Aljaž is a very good friend. I would say I know 90 per cent of the professionals although I haven't seen them in a while so it's going to be a lot of fun catching up with them.'

The Latvian Latin star was looking for a trusting type as her celebrity partner for this year's show. 'I truly admire all the celebrities for going out of their comfort zone. From them, the main thing is to be willing to learn, be open-minded and to have trust in me. Some professionals have been in the show for years and I am only just starting, but Patrick has to trust me so I can take him to the next level.'

She promises not to be too hard on her star pupil, though. 'I'm a tough teacher with a sense of humour. I come from a very difficult Russian school, but I consider myself more of an American type than a tough Russian girl.'

SETTING THE SCENE

It's mid-morning on the *Strictly* set, and the four finalists are about to make a dramatic entrance. The band strikes up a rousing rendition of 'The Final Countdown' as Dani, Kimberley, Denise and Louis pop out of a huge wooden box in the last few rehearsals.

Watching from the audience seats, and hoping the spectacular stunt goes without a hitch, is set designer **PATRICK DOHERTY** (above). 'We hired a four-man lift for the reveal of the finalists and there's an LED screen on the front of that, which will light up with graphics, so that's the big moment for us.

'With this, like all props, we have to get it off and on easily. Everything that comes in has to break down into sizeable bits to get off the studio floor. We have a 90-second break to dress the set while the training video plays, so it's a tight operation.'

The set, designed by Patrick in a revamp two years ago, has plenty of glitz and glamour, but for the Grand Final the team add a little extra sparkle. The staircases are hung with silver and the studio is dressed with silver drapes. The *Strictly* logo is wrapped around the glitterball and Tess's area is prepared for her

Crucial final checks are carried out before the dress rehearsal.

Pop-up celebs! The four finalists emerge from the toaster lift.

backstage interviews. But Saturday is relatively quiet for the set builders, who have put in the hard work earlier in the week. As the studio is used for other programmes in between shows, the set is broken down every Saturday night and rebuilt a few days later.

'The floor breaks into hundreds of pieces,' explains Patrick. 'Because it's not a standing set, the whole set has to break down. A couple of weeks ago they filmed a different programme here on a Wednesday night, so this set came in on Thursday morning and was up and ready to film on Friday afternoon.

'We have night crews, double crews, people working 24 hours a day. At the start of the series it's all in bits and takes about two weeks to put together but, once it's built, we can roll large sections in, bolt them together, and away we go.'

Patrick has worked on the programme since it was conceived, and he still loves coming up with new ideas every year. 'It is a show that has evolved,' he says. 'When we started ten years ago we had red drapes, a theatre arch and two staircases – and that was it. In 2010, when we redesigned the set, it really lifted the look and created more of an identity.'

The arches can have designs projected onto them, allowing the backdrop to change dramatically with minimal physical effort. 'Because there is such a small window of time, the arch is really important because it gives us a chance to change the look of the set. We don't have to bring in thousands of trees – we can put a forest in the background.'

For series 11, the show is moving from its original home at Television Centre to Elstree Studios, and a few adjustments will have to be made. 'The main difference is a bigger studio, which will enable us to pull the set apart and make the arch bigger. We'll have a bigger dance floor and more audience.'

Despite a decade on the show, watching hours of ballroom and Latin, Patrick is yet to pick up his dancing shoes. 'I've been here from the first year and I haven't learnt one step,' he laughs. 'Isn't that terrible!'

Vanessa FELTZ

Before the gruelling days of training with whip-cracker James Jordan, Vanessa will be facing early mornings on the Radio 2 Breakfast Show. But the hard-working broadcaster is happy to throw herself into learning new dances – for the sake of a new generation of audience.

'I am about to be a grandmother for the very first time and thought it would be wonderful to acquire a new skill at this advanced age,' she reveals. 'And it would be lovely to dance with a new baby.'

The TV presenter, broadcaster and journalist graduated from Cambridge University with a first-class honours degree, and went on to write for the *Daily Mirror*, present a radio show on the BBC's London station GLR and appear regularly on *The Big Breakfast*. In the 1990s she hosted her own talk show on ITV and then the BBC, and now writes a weekly column in the *Daily Express* as well as presenting her Radio 2 show.

Despite taking part in the BBC's *Let's Dance for Comic Relief* early this year, she claims she's no Ginger Rogers.

'I don't know how to dance,' she admits. 'I can't do any formal dances whatsoever. I can't jive, I can't salsa, I can't cha-cha-cha, I can't waltz – I just can't dance at all really so I'd have to say, out of ten, I'd be a one. Although from a one the only way is up … unless I fall over, then the only way is down!'

The forthright 51 year old may well bite back if she gets a lashing from the judges, but she is hoping they will like her routines.

'I'd like them to say that I tried hard and that I mastered the dance, and that I don't look like a fool,' she laughs. 'I don't want them to say that they are affronted or disgusted or appalled, that I look like a tugboat in full sail, that I look like a bull in a china shop. I want them to say that I look like a dancer dancing. If they say that, I will be thrilled to pieces.'

Known for her strong personality, she may also prove a match for fiery James, but she promises to behave – if only so she doesn't show herself up.

'If I sprinkle a little light entertainment into the lives of the nation during this terrible recession, they will only thank me for it,' she says. 'But I don't want to disgrace my family so I am going to work hard and do as I'm told.'

James
JORDAN

James's seventh outing on *Strictly* brought him tantalisingly close to the glitterball with Denise Van Outen. The former presenter turned out to be a formidable talent and their incredible lifts in the showdance had the audience – and the judges – gasping with astonishment. But they lost at the final hurdle to Olympic medallist Louis Smith.

'Being partnered with Denise was great because we both have such similar personalities and share the same sense of humour,' he says. 'We were always laughing in training and the whole experience was pure fun. Series 10 was amazing for me. I really got to push myself as a dancer and that's all down to having a hard-working celebrity. We became really good friends.'

As the son of two dance teachers, the Kent-born star grew up with ballroom in his blood but was reluctant to take it up at the age of 11, when his parents encouraged him. However, talent will out and he started competing at 15, becoming one of the best in the world by the time he was 21. After meeting Ola in Poland, in 2000, he began dancing, and romancing, with her and they waltzed down the aisle together in 2003.

Having spent last season at the top of the leader board, James was always hoping for a partner to match Denise's skills, as well as someone he can have fun with.

'First and foremost I would like someone I can get on with,' he says. 'When you're spending eight hours a day with a celebrity, you want to be on the same wavelength. Secondly, I want someone I can push and who will test me as a choreographer.'

As well as being a passionate and sometimes fiery teacher, James is fiercely ambitious and sets his sights high.

'I am very competitive, there's no denying the fact, so for me, satisfaction wise, to get to the final is a wonderful thing. It took me a while but I've done it twice now.

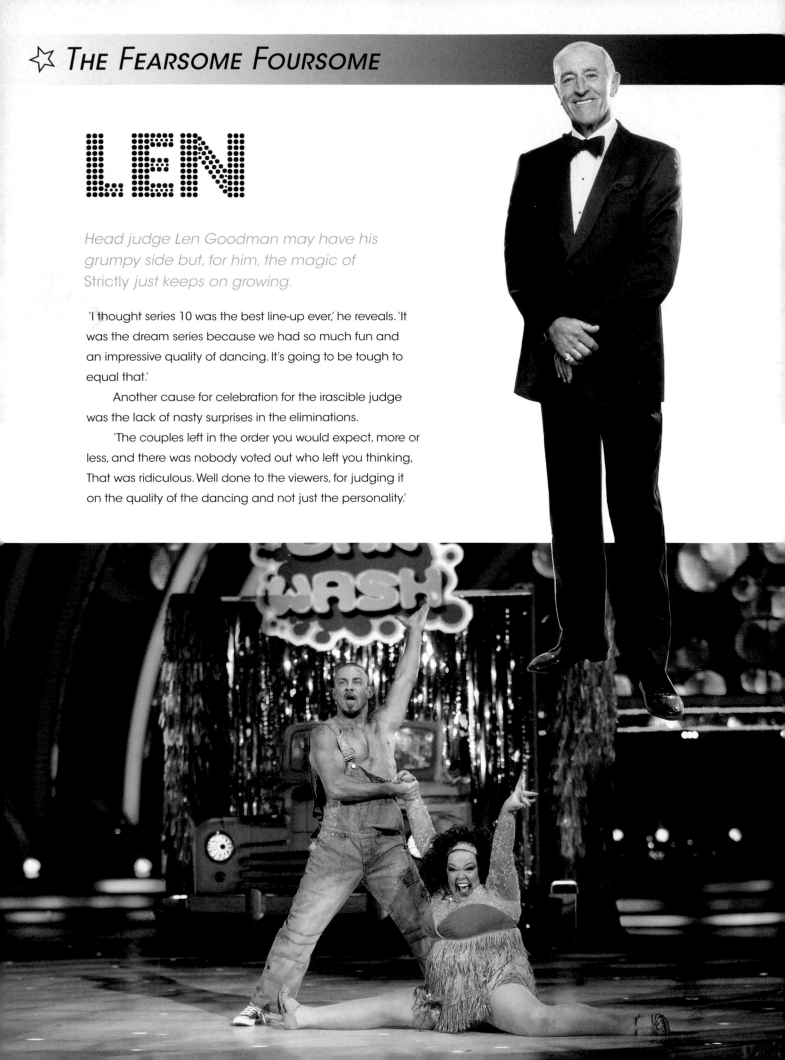

LEN

Head judge Len Goodman may have his grumpy side but, for him, the magic of Strictly just keeps on growing.

'I thought series 10 was the best line-up ever,' he reveals. 'It was the dream series because we had so much fun and an impressive quality of dancing. It's going to be tough to equal that.'

Another cause for celebration for the irascible judge was the lack of nasty surprises in the eliminations.

'The couples left in the order you would expect, more or less, and there was nobody voted out who left you thinking, That was ridiculous. Well done to the viewers, for judging it on the quality of the dancing and not just the personality.'

Opposite below: Lisa Riley sparkles in her 'Car Wash' samba. **Above:** Going for gold: The finalists pop up for a close-run competition

Who improved the most?

Nicky Byrne tended to lack confidence at the beginning, but as the show went along his confidence rose and a couple of his dances were absolutely terrific.

Was Louis a worthy winner?

He probably was, but I wouldn't have been disappointed if Denise Van Outen had won. She was the most rounded dancer of the finalists.

However, I understand that Louis was popular and he was a hunky guy, so I was happy with the result. Kimberley was fabulous. As far as the judges were concerned there was a hair's breadth between the three of them.

You're moving studios this year; how do you feel about that?

It's a mixed blessing. It will take another 100 or so in the audience so hopefully there'll be a bit more of an atmosphere. However, it's further away from where I live so, from my own point of view, I'd rather stay put! But that's just me being selfish!

Favourite dance of the series?

Without a doubt, Denise's Charleston to 'Walk Like an Egyptian'. That was fabulous. It's probably the best Charleston there's ever been on the show.

How did Darcey do as a judge?

I think she did marvellously well. Myself, Craig and Bruno have done this for years, so it's difficult to walk in and become one of the judges, and she brought a different dynamic to the panel. She talked about the artistry of the dance, which is what you'd expect, and she did really well.

Who was the biggest surprise?

Lisa. Smiley Riley. That's the charm of *Strictly* – when you looked at the list of runners and riders at the start you would have thought that she's not a natural dancer, but she was wonderful. If anyone epitomised the joy of dance it was Lisa. She went for it 100 per cent and she and Robin had wonderful chemistry together. When you see somebody having such a wonderful time, it's infectious. Lisa doing the splits, at the end of her Wembley dance, was an iconic moment.

Dave MYERS

The Hairy Biker is hoping he'll be cooking with gas on the dance floor and says he had no hesitation in accepting the *Strictly* invitation. 'It's a lovely programme,' he says. 'I genuinely enjoy the show and it's very flattering to be asked. It didn't take too long to think about it really.'

Dave and screen partner Simon King cooked their way into the nation's heart with their *Hairy Bikers* series, travelling around the world on a quest for great recipes. A series of recipe books by the hirsute chefs have made them the third most popular cookery-book writers in the UK. But before launching the hit show Dave racked up an interesting CV, working as a furnaceman in a steelworks to finance his master's degree in Fine Arts, before joining the BBC as a make-up artist to specialise in prosthetics.

But what does biker Simon think of his latest venture? 'He thinks I'm nuts!' laughs Dave. 'He just thinks it's really funny. We've been mates for 20 years and we've always said with anything that comes up, "Just give it a go". We've had some mad schemes over the years, and we egg each other on.

'I think it suited Si as well because he was desperate for some time off. It's odd when you're half of a double act. It's hard to make that decision, because you think about the other person, and this has fallen at the right time for him. I miss him though, after ten years of the *Hairy Bikers*.'

Due to his recent series, the *Hairy Dieters*, Dave has lost 3 stone before even hitting the dance floor. But he's not in a hurry to lose much more. 'I'm not on a diet at the moment, but I am practising what I'm preaching – day-to-day healthy eating,' he says. 'I love Japanese food and Thai food. I'm living on a barge on the Thames when I'm down here and I've got my wok going there, it's great.'

Despite Bruno's launch-show comment that he looked like a 'final-destination car crash', the fun-loving foodie is working on a recipe for success – with help from dance partner Karen Hauer. 'I think I'm going to be worked very hard, which is fine,' he says. 'If I work hard maybe I can fend that car crash off for a couple of weeks, which would be lovely!'

Karen HAUER

Last year the Venezuelan beauty was the only new girl, but she certainly impressed – whipping a nervous Nicky Byrne into shape and getting him to the quarter-finals. Despite his tentative first steps, Karen thought he was the ideal partner for her debut outing on the show.

'Having been partnered with Nicky Byrne on my first series of *Strictly*, it set the standard of what a great partnership should be like,' she says. 'He was fun, focused and ready to perform at all times.'

Karen was born in Valencia, Venezuela, and moved to New York with her family aged eight. It was then that she was chosen to study African dance, after doing the splits in an audition – in a pair of jeans! Two years later she won a scholarship to the Martha Graham School of Contemporary Dance, where she danced for ten years before moving on to 'Fame School' at LaGuardia High School of Performing Arts for dance, majoring in ballet and contemporary.

At 19, she went to a cha-cha-cha class and fell in love with Latin dance and soon became the American Rhythm National Champion and World Mambo Champion. She has also worked as a dancer for Jennifer Lopez and danced on *So You Think You Can Dance*.

Joining *Strictly* last year was a dream come true for the Latin beauty and she admits to a few nerves.

'Series 10 was like a roller coaster,' she remembers. 'It was exciting and made me have more than just one butterfly in my stomach! I did things I had never dreamed of and all the time watched by millions of loving and supportive *Strictly* fans.'

This year comes with an added bonus – she will be joined on the *Strictly* team by her British fiancée Kevin Clifton. But when it comes to her celebrity partner, Karen is open-minded.

'Every type of celebrity – sports guy, singer, actor – has their own advantages,' she reasons. 'For example, an athlete is always on the go and actors are very dramatic, so you can work with different things. I just try to make the best of it and bring out their strengths.

'I can get on with anybody who works hard – and of course, if they bring me chocolate and coffee, then I'm happy!' So her pairing with food-fanatic Dave is surely a recipe for success.

ACROSS

7. Karen _____, dancer who was paired up with Nicky Byrne in her first series (5)

8. Latin-dance specialist who won series 7 with Chris Hollins (3, 6)

9. Brucie's co-host (4, 4)

10. _____ Britton, TV presenter who partnered Artem in Series 10 and on tour (4)

11. _____ Jordan, husband of 8A, who's twice reached the final – with Pamela Stevenson and Denise Van Outen (5)

12. _____ Chambers, actor who partnered Camilla to her only series win (3)

14. Denise _____, athlete who finished runner-up to Jill Halfpenny in 2004 (5)

16. Siobhan _____, actress who went out in week 1 with Matthew Cutler in 2005 (5)

17. _____ Widdecombe, *Strictly* favourite who, with Anton, took on Russell Grant and Flavia for *Children in Need* (3)

18. Karen _____, *It Takes Two* regular who also partnered cricketer Mark Ramprakash to sizzling victory in series 4 (5)

23. _____ Tointon, ex-*EastEnders* star who won Strictly with Artem (4)

24. Former *Emmerdale* star who didn't quite make it to the final with Robin (4, 5)

26 & 13D. Cyclist who made it to week 7 with Brendan (8,9)

27. Emma _____, former Spice Girl who reached the final with Darren Bennett (6)

DOWN

1. Former gymnast and *Blue Peter* presenter who competed in the 2010 final (4, 5)

2. _____ Wallace, *EastEnders* star who lost in a dance-off to Heather Small in 2008 (6)

3. See 22D

4. _____ Virshilas, dancer who partnered sportsmen Phil Tufnell and 20D (5)

5. _____ Ball, 2005 finalist who succeeded Claudia as host of *It Takes Two* (3)

6. _____ Judd, drummer who scored two perfect 40s to win the final in Blackpool in 2011 (5)

10. _____ Phillips, former daytime presenter who lasted till week 4 with Brendan in series 3 (5)

13. See 26A

15. Dancer who partnered 5D, 14A and 21D (3, 5)

19. Dancer who was not able to partner Johnny Ball because of injury (6)

20. Welsh rugby player who made it as far as the semis in 2010 (5)

21. _____ Paris, singer and presenter who only got to week 2 in 2006 (4)

22 & 3D Sports presenter who, with 11A, competed against their respective spouses, Kenny and 8A, in 2007 (5, 5)

25. 'When Doves _____', song to which Pasha and Kimberley danced the tango in the final (3)

Strictly INTERNATIONAL

```
E L L B R E N D A N C O L E F P P
U N A D R O J A L O O E A L O U A
R N G N N A L A H C K L A L R A S
A N E L U I I A O E A V A E N U H
O L N W A T L L B E I N L A K P A
S R I A Z N R U A A D L K A A E K
E U I O E E D O C R A A R I Z A O
W S Y N N A A F D T E V I A L V
O S A L O A C L A N N S B E K E A
L I E T A A V L A H A C U A H U L
E A N R C T L I A N R I E A S Z E
I A C E E I I U L L D H R S T E V
L I H F M D E N M A R K A B A N A
A V N A O R A K H W N T A D N E Z
T A C T L I T H U A N I A V A V D
A A L S E T A T S D E T I N U T E
N T K A T Y A V I R S H I L A S L
```

Strictly Come Dancing is an international competition with dancers from all over the world taking part. Listed below are 11 dancers and the country where they were born. Can you find them all in the grid and then match up each dancer with their nation of origin? Turn to page 65 for the solutions.

DANCERS

ALIONA VILANI
ANTON DU BEKE
BRENDAN COLE
BRIAN FORTUNA
CAMILLA DALLERUP
FLAVIA CACACE
KAREN HAUER
KATYA VIRSHILAS
NATALIE LOWE
OLA JORDAN
PASHA KOVALEV

COUNTRIES

AUSTRALIA
DENMARK
ENGLAND
ITALY
KAZAKHSTAN
LITHUANIA
NEW ZEALAND
POLAND
RUSSIA
UNITED STATES
VENEZUELA

From the pairing of the celebs on the launch show to Louis's last leap towards the glitterball in the Grand Final, series 10 was packed with fun – both on and off the dance floor. We've been leafing through the family album to choose a few of our golden moments from 2012 – caught on camera.

STRICTLY SNAPSHOT

Leaping to victory! Finalist Louis Smith is having the Time of His Life in his *Dirty Dancing* salsa. The Olympic medallist rounded off an incredible 2012 by clinching the title of *Strictly Come Dancing* champ, with Flavia Cacace, beating off competion from Dani, Denise and Kimberley in a closely fought final.

Halloween night saw ghouls, ghosts and demons ruling the dance floor in a costume extravanganza. Dani and Vincent showed they could Scooby Doo a cha-cha-cha and bag 27 points – and they would have got away with the top of the leader board … if it hadn't been for those pesky five couples in front.

Flasher Fern: In week 6, charlady Fern Britton refused to keep it clean and, after a quick going-over of the judges with a feather duster, showed them what she was really made of. But shaking her tail feather failed to keep her in, and the audience vote polished her off.

Nicky Byrne's turn at Wembley made his knees go all trembly – Elvis style. The former Westlife star began his 'Jailhouse Rock' jive on the judges' desk on an evening that brought the show to an audience of 6,000, and saw Denise Van Outen bag 39 for her Egyptian Charleston. The little sphinx.

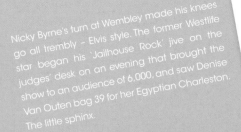

Lisa Riley made the judges 'Think' when she exploded on to the show in week 1 with a lively cha-cha-cha to the Aretha Franklin classic. And she proved she was the muscles of the partnership when Robin happily jumped into her arms.

Can he kick it? Yes he cancan! Spruce Bruce proved he's still got what it takes when he pulled off a high-kicking routine with some leggy showgirls in week 5. Go Brucie!

Let's Dance! New judge Darcey Bussell burst into the *Strictly* fold in a sparkling launch video that saw her dance ballroom with Bruno, get Craig on his toes for a show-stopping twirl and put a twinkle in Len's eye with a tasty tango.

It's Raining 10s! Kimberley and Pasha clinch the first 40 in the quarter-finals. Their cha-cha-cha/tango fusion to 'It's Raining Men' had Len on his feet for a standing ovation, and Bruno declaring, 'You started a nuclear fusion.'

Craig Revel Horwood got into the spirit of the Hollywood special by clanking over to the judges' table, dressed as the Tin Man from *The Wizard of Oz*. If he only had a heart!

You've Got a Friend in Me! James and Denise go to 'infinity and beyond' with their *Toy Story* foxtrot.

Deborah MEADEN

The *Dragons' Den* star is hoping to add some fire to the dance floor – and slay the opposition. But she's set herself a tough target from the start.

'About a week before I said I would do the show I did an interview and said, "I would love to have done *Strictly* but I will never ever do anything I can't win." That's going to come back and bite me,' she quips. 'But they asked me and *Strictly* is *Strictly*. Sometimes my life is spent making decisions on what's the right and the wrong thing to do, and I just thought, D'you know what? I'm going to do it.

'It's an amazing opportunity and I would not be able to live with myself if I didn't do it. I thought I would absolutely regret this more than anything if I didn't take part.'

The multi-millionaire businesswoman proved a successful entrepreneur from a young age, launching a glass-and-ceramics export company before setting up one of the first Stefanel fashion franchises in the UK and going on to build up a portfolio of companies in the retail-and-leisure sector. In 2003, she became a household name as one of five investors on *Dragons' Den* and now devotes time to finding good investment opportunities. And while she's prepared to invest her time in training, she was forced to tell dance partner Robin Windsor 'I'm out', at least for the first week of rehearsals.

'I feel terrible because I had a week's holiday booked and wasn't able to train for the first week. After that, I promised Robin, I would do two solid weeks of nothing but dancing, ten-plus hours a day. We're still negotiating that.'

Although Deborah says she was 'atrocious' at ballroom classes at school, she got a taste of the *Strictly* experience when she did *Let's Dance for Comic Relief* with fellow Dragons Peter Jones and Duncan Bannatyne.

'I loved it,' she recalls. 'Anton judged it. He said "Deborah, you have lovely arms." That's all he could think of saying. Then he looked at the other boys, then back at me and said, "Deborah you have lovely arms."'

As well as the dancing the no-nonsense 54 year old is looking forward to the sparkly frocks and Saturday night makeovers.

'What girl wouldn't?' she laughs. 'For the launch show, I had six people stood around me doing hair and make-up. It was completely fabulous.'

Robin WINDSOR

Before embarking on the last series, Robin's biggest wish was for someone who could match the 'wonderful and lovely' Anita Dobson for enthusiasm. The mission seemed strictly impossible – until Robin was paired with the bubbly bundle of fun that is Lisa Riley. She also helped him break his week 9 curse, by dancing him into the semi-finals.

'Dancing with Lisa last year was absolutely amazing,' he says. 'It was the campest time of my life! Lisa brought joy to the nation and I have made a friend for life. If one sentence could sum it all up it would be "Never judge a book by its cover".'

Robin was an early starter, taking his first dance classes at the age of three. He won his first tournament aged 11 and had represented England at numerous international competitions by the time he was a teenager. In 2002, Robin joined *Burn the Floor*, where he danced for nine years, along with dance partner Kristina Rihanoff. He joined *Strictly* in 2010.

Robin loves the thrill of the live show on Saturday night, but he keeps his own butterflies in check while he deals with the inevitable jitters of his partner.

'Nerves take over on the night,' he explains. 'At the end of the day you're there with your celebrity and it's your job to nurture them, because they are nervous. They are out of their comfort zone, doing something they're not used to in front of 12 million people, and your main priority is them.'

The Ipswich-born dancer reveals that, despite their close relationship, there is always a little rivalry among the pros on Saturday night.

'We find that sports stars are a little more competitive because they're driven and it's what they've grown up doing. It's the same for us professionals: we are there to do a job but we are all competitive because we come from a competitive background. At the same time we are one big family, and we all still like to look after one another.'

Ashley TAYLOR DAWSON

If perfect timing is the key to *Strictly* success, the *Hollyoaks* heartthrob doesn't stand much chance – his fiancée, Karen, is due to give birth to their second child in the early weeks of the show. 'I'm the busiest I've ever been in *Hollyoaks*, and I'm having a baby around the time of the first main show so everything's easy,' he jokes. 'It's really good timing.'

The 31-year-old actor – who has been paired with Ola Jordan for the show – admits it is going to be tough-going for the first few weeks, juggling a new addition to the family with his new dancer's regime.

But the real problem will come if Ashley junior decides to arrive in the middle of a live show on Saturday night.

'I don't know what to do about that – I'm trying not to think about it,' says the anguished father-to-be. 'It's the ultimate dilemma!'

Ashley is best known as bad lad Darren Osborne in the Channel 4 soap. Born in Wilmslow, he got his first acting break at 17 with the National Youth Theatre, before joining *Hollyoaks* in 1999. Although he's never studied ballroom, he has done a bit of singing and dancing, as a member of the band allSTARS*, from 2001 to 2003.

Ashley is 'over the moon' to be partnered with Ola and is not concerned that his pin-up looks will make James jealous. 'It makes it all the better because he's been teasing me since I got here,' he laughs. 'Now I can get my own back.'

The actor has been learning some gymnastics in the run-up to the show. 'I want to try it and I want to push myself, whether I can dance or not,' he says. 'I just want to enjoy it and do the best I can. If I go out early I wouldn't be gutted for the winning or the losing, I'd be gutted because I wouldn't be trying every single dance and really furthering my experience.'

Ashley follows former *Hollyoaks* stars Ali Bastian and Ricky Whittle on to the dance floor, and reckons he has a lot to live up to.

'They raised the bar right up there,' he says. 'They both got to at least the semi-final so ... nice one, cheers, guys!'

Ola JORDAN

Former champ Ola Jordan looked like she was in for a few weeks of fun when she was paired with cheeky chappy Sid Owen for series 10. But their *Ghostbusters* cha-cha-cha on Halloween night proved a bit ghoulish and they were eliminated in week 3.

'Sid was a fabulous partner,' she insists. 'He was so sweet and outgoing. We got on from the moment we met. I had so much fun with him during every rehearsal; it was just a shame we left the competition at an early stage. Last series was amazing but this year – bring it on!'

The Polish dancer was singled out as a raw talent by her tutor, after starting lessons at school in Warsaw at 12. And, at the age of 17, she won the Open Polish Championship of Dance and was placed in the top 12 in the World Championships.

In March 2000, when Ola was looking for a new partner, James Jordan flew to Poland for a try-out – and clearly liked what he saw. They soon became partners, on and off the dance floor, and were married three years later.

Ola's amazing teaching skills saw her turn breakfast-TV presenter Chris Hollins into a *Strictly* winner, but she admits that some celebs might be beyond her magical powers. 'You can't make everyone an amazing dancer,' she says. 'You try your best and, for me, when they walk into the room and I see the way they stand, the way they walk, I can see if they are going to be any good or not.

'Most of my celebrities have never had any dance training before. I've had a lot of sports stars who've never danced or acted, so some of them are quite hard work. But I think that's what makes me a good teacher and makes me work hard. So it's good for me and feels like an achievement for me as a teacher when they do well.'

Despite coming close on a couple of occasions, husband James has yet to pick up the main prize – and Ola says she has him polishing her trophy at home.

'That's James's job every day,' she laughs. 'But, seriously, he's been brilliant. There is a competitive side to us and we're always winding each other up, but that's us. We like teasing each other. But he's very helpful, he helps me, so I help him.

'If it's not me going home with the trophy this year, I would love it to be James.'

THE FINAL COUNTDOWN

On final day, timing is tight, and every step has to be on schedule. During the build-up to the live show, the studio corridors buzz with excitement as the whole team pull together to bring their faithful audience an unforgettable grand finale. We crept backstage at the series 10 final to get a minute-by-minute lowdown on this very special day.

Rain dance! Loyal *Strictly* fans brave the weather for the final.

The professionals rehearse for the opening number.

9.45 a.m. It would take more than cold weather and persistent rain to keep the hardy *Strictly* fans away. A queue of raincoats and umbrellas has already formed outside Television Centre, and the weather isn't dampening any spirits. That's dedication!

10.00 a.m. The long day is just beginning, but the professional dancers are already on the floor, rehearsing the opening dance in gold-and-white costumes. The four finalists – Kimberley, Dani, Denise and Louis – will pop up like magic from a huge black-and-silver box during the dance.

10.30 a.m. The 'toaster lift' used in the reveal of the finalists is taken apart and wheeled offstage to make way for the couples to rehearse for the last time before the dress run.

10.45 a.m. Dani and Vincent are first on the floor. The schedule is so tight that the couples are only allowed 10 minutes' rehearsal time for each dance to add to the 15 minutes they were allowed in the studio on the previous day.

10.55 a.m. Denise and James are the next couple to take their rehearsal slot. Denise is looking every inch the dancer in skin-tight black Lycra, from head to toe, but the show dance is proving tough. James has choreographed plenty of impressive lifts, but both are injured.

'I dislocated a rib on Thursday in rehearsal for the show dance, and it's a bit sore,' Denise reveals later. 'I've had it popped back in but it does hurt. I'm not having any physio because you can't touch it. There's not a lot you can do other than take painkillers and keep moaning about it!

'James has also dislocated his shoulder. You get tired over the weeks of training and it's then that injuries happen.'

11 a.m. Dani is in hair, enjoying a rare sit-down and looking forward to this evening's performance. 'Amazingly, it's quite relaxed this week, because we haven't got anything to lose any more,' she says. 'It's the last day. And we all want to go out there and have fun.'

Pocket rockets: Dani and Vincent in final rehearsals.

Working through the pain: Denise and James practise the show dance.

11.15 a.m. Kimberley rehearses her show dance. Wearing a jumpsuit, she pops behind a circle of opaque paper, which then bursts into 10-foot flames to reveal the singer in a skimpy Latin outfit.

Due to the cost of the flash-paper circles, there are only three available – one for rehearsal, one for dress run and one for the live show – so this is the first time she and Pasha have used the real thing. Kimberley is understandably nervous, but chalks it down to another amazing *Strictly Come Dancing* experience.

'I just hope we can make it work on the night,' she explains. 'There are a lot of exciting things going on in our show dance. It's the quickest change I've ever done, and I'm nervous, but really excited at the same time.'

12.00 p.m. Dani and Vincent are practising their tango. Some familiar faces appear in the studio corridor as the former contestants begin to gather for one final dance.

The girls arrive first, with Fern Britton, Lisa Riley and Victoria Pendleton chatting in the 'star bar' – the backstage hospitality area – where soft drinks, fruit and piles of chocolate have been laid on to keep the hard-working dancers and celebs in much needed fuel for the day ahead.

12.30 p.m. Louis and Flavia are grabbing some last-minute practice in the corridor. The rest of the eliminated contestants are greeting each other like long-lost friends.

'Coming back is just so lovely,' Fern says. 'It's like meeting your family again when you've been away for a few weeks.'

The TV presenter also reveals a little *Strictly* secret. 'I have a little box at home full of all my *Strictly* memories. I've collected every pair of false eyelashes I ever wore, little bits of twinkle that have fallen off each costume. I've got all the handwritten notes from the runners who looked after me; all sorts of bits and pieces. Artem gave

Harmer chameleon: Dani's hair is transformed for the show dance.

Anton and Sid share a laugh in the star bar before the show begins.

me some roses when we finished so I dried the petals, and I've got those in a little bag.'

While she's delighted to be reunited with partner Artem, Fern is not pining for their training sessions. 'I don't miss him being cross with me,' she laughs. 'My brain is not tuned to that thinking pattern of counting and positions and feet shapes; so I frustrated him because I didn't get everything straight away.'

1.22 p.m. The returning celebs are on the dance floor, rehearsing with the professionals for their group dance to 'River Deep Mountain High'.

Louis is in the star bar with a heat pad strapped to his back because of an injury, but he's looking forward to his three dances. 'I'm knackered but excited,' he says. 'A lot of the dances have bits that can go wrong, like splits and somersaults, but if it goes well I'll be very happy.'

1.30 p.m. All the dancers and celebrities are wandering in and out of the star bar as lunch is served.

Sid Owen is chatting to Michael Vaughan and Anton as the excitement builds, ahead of the dress run. 'It's going to be a great show, very tight,' predicts Sid. 'Nobody can call it, so it should be really exciting. The four finalists are all good. They're all worthy winners.'

Sid admits he was disappointed to be knocked out at week 3, but adds, 'That's the way it goes. It is a tough competition. I loved every bit of it. I certainly wouldn't shy away from dancing now so it's given me confidence.'

2.30 p.m. The dress run begins, and Bruce and Tess introduce the four final couples. Denise and James kick off with their 'Tutti Frutti' jive and are then ushered over to the judges' desk. Four crew members – who have taken the place of the judges for the rehearsal – cause a ripple of laughter with their passable impressions of Craig, Darcey, Len and Bruno.

Costume, hair and make-up have decamped to the star bar to practise the quick changes needed between dances.

Say cheese! Returning contestants pose for a final snap in the Star Bar..

Final farewell: Sid and Ola have one last fling in the group dance.

3.35 p.m. The dress run for the first show ends, and there is a 10-minute turnaround for the stage crew to prepare for the live results show, while the band and dancers take a short break.

3.45 p.m. All four couples perform their favourite dance from the series for the last time before the real thing. On the night, only three will get to dance, as one couple will be eliminated. At the end of the dress run, Bruce declares Denise and James the winners to practise the handover of the glitterball, but they refuse to take it, for fear of jinxing their chances.

4.35 p.m. Dress rehearsal over, the crew are making the set ready for the live show. The hosts, professionals and celebrities head off to grab a hot dinner in the star bar or in their dressing rooms. Kimberley, Denise and Dani head back to hair and make-up to be restyled for their first look of the live show. The judges are arriving, with Len the first to appear.

5 p.m. The studio is beginning to buzz as an excited audience files in from the main bar where they have been held while they waited. The ladies shimmer in glitzy outfits, and everyone has adhered to the glamorous dress code. It wouldn't be *Strictly* unless the dedicated studio audience sparkled almost as much as the dancers!

6.15 p.m. Bruce is on stage for his warm-up. This is one of his favourite parts of the show, and he's on top form, getting the audience in the mood with his gags. One lucky lady gets pulled on to her feet to dance with him, and he shows off some pretty fancy footwork.

6.25 p.m. Backstage, there is frenzied activity in the star bar. Kimberley sits at the dressing table with five people putting the last-minute touches to her hair and make-up.

A runner shouts for the returning celebrities to 'Go to Tess's area.' Denise walks through, looking

Jinx: Bruce tries to award the trophy in rehearsal but no one wants to play glitterball.

Show time! Dani gets the finishing touches to her make up.

understandably shattered, but ready and raring to go in her red-dotted jive dress any minute.

6.30 p.m. And we're off. The professional dancers take to the floor to the strains of Europe's hit 'The Final Countdown' as the eyes of the four celebrity finalists flash across an LED screen on the front of the toaster lift. As the four remaining celebrities – Kimberley, Dani, Denise and Louis – pop up, the audience go wild with appreciation.

6.55 p.m. Denise has performed her jive and managed to land an impressive 39 points. But there's no time to rest on her laurels, and she's backstage for a 10-minute change before her show dance. Two tents have been erected in the star bar for changing, and she whips into a black-lace catsuit. As soon as she sits down at the mirror, the hair stylists and make-up artists swoop. Her hair is soon up, her make-up altered, and she's ready to go back onstage.

James is gearing up for the lifts in the show dance, despite the shoulder injury and a torn ligament in his foot. 'If I were a footballer I'd be out for weeks, but dancers are hardcore,' he jokes. 'There are loads of lifts, but I know I only have to do it one more time; so I can pull it out of the bag.'

7.10 p.m. While Louis and Flavia are earning a 39 with their salsa, Kimberley is changing into the jumpsuit she'll shed behind the flaming hoop in one of the many show-stopping moments of the final. Then her hair is let down, tousled and sprayed into a wild, wanton look.

7.20 p.m. Denise and James take to the dance floor to perform their show dance – pulling off six amazing lifts and a floor-spin before Denise ends in the splits. Full marks and an appraisal of 'epic' from Bruno.

7.30 p.m. Dani and Vincent are on the floor for a dramatic show dance to 'Bohemian Rhapsody'. They land 35 and an 'intoxicating' from Craig.

Denise gets Tutti Frutti with James in the jive.

What a Feeling! Denise and James celebrate a successful show dance.

7.35 p.m. Kimberley's fiery show dance – to Beyoncé's 'Crazy in Love' – goes without a hitch and is deemed 'smoking hot' by Bruno, landing a 39.

7.42 p.m. Louis makes a topless and barefoot entrance with a power handstand on a huge globe. He has the *Strictly* world in the palm of his hand and nabs a perfect score. 'If this show goes on for another 20 years we'll never see another show dance as magical as that,' says Len.

7.55 p.m. The dancers and celebs head backstage during the break between live shows. They swoop on the piles of mini-choc bars and bananas in a bid to replace the well-spent energy. Richard Arnold is in his element, chatting and laughing with new pal Michael Vaughan, thrilled to be back in the *Strictly* fold.

'I've never had an experience like it because I'm not a natural performer,' he says. 'I've been on live TV, but I've never been on a show like this, never felt the heat of the lights and smelt the greasepaint; so to be part of this has been an extraordinary adventure for me. It's brought me such joy.'

He paid tribute to his dance partner, saying, 'I don't know what I'd do without Erin. When I left I thought I'd have to call her to find out which foot went first when I was crossing the road!' She's not the only glamorous pal he's picked up, either. 'I have Jerry Hall's mobile number, and she's invited me to her house in Texas, which is all very rock and roll,' he confides. 'But I do make a mean margarita!'

8.20 p.m. The eliminated celebs head back to the studio for their final group dance. Lisa Riley, who was knocked out in the semi-finals, is bubbling over with her usual enthusiasm.

'It's been so long since we were all together; so to have the whole team here is gorgeous,' she says. 'Hair and make-up have told us that never before have they seen such camaraderie among the contestants. The whole thing has been insane, but it's been great.'

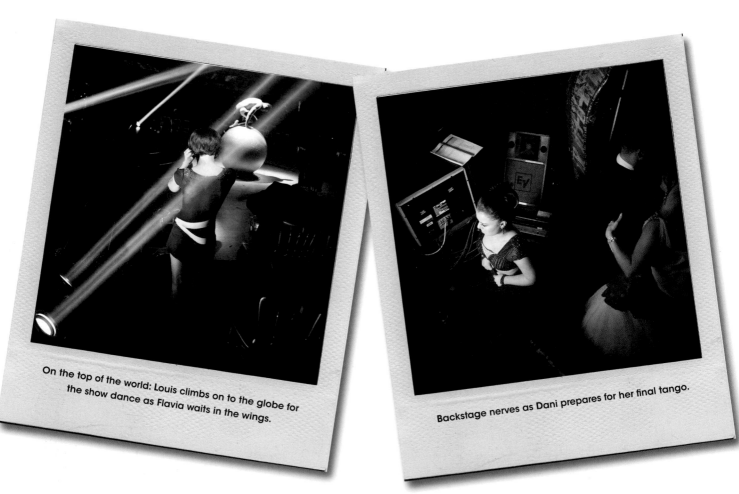

On the top of the world: Louis climbs on to the globe for the show dance as Flavia waits in the wings.

Backstage nerves as Dani prepares for her final tango.

8.45 p.m. The runners are earning their keep, making sure everyone is in place for the final show. With the first elimination looming and one more dance for the remaining couples, there is a mixture of tension and relief in the star bar. Louis reveals he is almost as nervous as the first time he took to the floor.

'They are two very different types of pressure,' he says. 'The first-ever week it was so nerve-racking because I'd never done anything like that before. Now it's the expectation, and this being the last-ever episode; so it's a very different sort of night.'

Being one step closer to picking up the prize, Kimberley insists she doesn't mind who triumphs on the night. 'Everyone deserves to win. None of us really is too worried about how it turns out; we just want to do a good job with our own performances.'

8.50 p.m. All is quiet backstage as the results show begins. For costume, make-up and hair, the quick changes are all over, and it's time to relax – and clear away their many tools of the trade. The glitterball is on the stage as the first couple to leave the final learn their fate. It's Dani and Vincent.

9.25 p.m. After full marks were picked up for Kimberley's 'Strictly irresistible' tango and Denise's Egyptian Charleston – which Craig declared 'simply the best Charleston we've ever, ever had' – Louis gets 39 for his own favourite Charleston. Craig's score of 9 sparks a round of boos from the audience that drowns out Tess.

9.55 p.m. Flavia holds back the tears as she and Louis are crowned *Strictly* champs.

10.05 p.m. Flavia and Louis are showered in congratulations, and there are hugs all round, as everyone prepares to say goodbye.

After 3 months of tears, triumphs and a whole lot of camaraderie, the 14 exhausted celebs and professionals head off for a well-deserved Christmas break. It's all over for another year.

Champions! Louis and Flavia lift the trophy after a close contest for first place.

No hard feelings: the finalists unite to congratulate Louis after his win.

Rachel RILEY

The *Countdown* star is swapping the mathematical numbers for musical ones, but her legendary arithmetic skills could still come in handy when she's counting the steps. Paired with two-time finalist Pasha Kovalev, Rachel reckons it all adds up.

'It doesn't worry me that he's reached the final both times he's been in the show,' she says. 'Everyone keeps coming up to me and saying congratulations because I got Pasha, so I'm really happy. We'll get on fine because he's such a gentleman – and he likes chocolate!'

Oxford graduate Rachel was chosen from over a thousand applicants to become *Countdown* queen in 2009, despite having no television experience. She has since filmed over 1,000 programmes and has also become a presenter on *The Gadget Show*.

Although she loves a boogie, Rachel is starting from scratch when it comes to ballroom. 'I'm first up at weddings and parties but there's dancing and there's dancing,' she laughs. 'I'm not even going to show you those moves!' Now she is hoping Pasha can teach her to be 'elegant'.

'I'm looking forward to starting, and I think it will be really good fun,' she says. '*Strictly* is the opportunity that you just don't turn down. I have never danced before, I only had one hour of dancing lessons before my wedding, but it really appeals to get the chance to be taught how to be graceful and elegant by professionals.

'As my friends know, I'm really clumsy and I have never been graceful in my life so maybe now is the time to start.'

Rachel has been keeping an eye on her fellow contestants and says it won't all be about the dance level they are starting at.

'I was staring at Natalie for most of the launch showdance, before I went on, just thinking, Wow, she's amazing. But whatever level you are you've got to improve and the viewers like to see that. I love watching Dave and I think the viewers are going to fall in love with him. You've got to put your heart and soul into it, work hard and have fun.'

Wardrobe-wise Rachel is keen to embrace the *Strictly* style but has already come up against a painful problem.

'There is one pair of shoes I'd like to put on a bonfire,' she admits. 'My first pair of shoes were great and then these came and within 5 minutes, I had a blister. I'm already suffering for my art!'

Pasha
KOVALEV

Pasha has made a massive impact in his first two years – making it to the final and finishing as runner-up with both Chelsee Healey and Kimberley Walsh. This year he is hoping to take that final step towards the glitterball – but his new partner, Rachel, has a lot to live up to.

'Dancing with Kimberley was fantastic,' he says. 'She was the perfect partner and I couldn't believe my luck when it was revealed I'd be dancing with her.

Born in Siberia, Pasha was introduced to ballroom by his mum, who took him to watch a competition when he was eight. He was immediately hooked, and trained hard to win Russian competitions before moving to the States, where he became a US National Latin finalist, an Ohio Star Ball finalist and also reached the finals of *So You Think You Can Dance* in the US. He also performed in the Broadway and West End productions of *Burn the Floor* and has taught all styles of ballroom including International Standard, American smooth and rhythm, but his specialty is International Latin.

Being asked to join the show, in series 9, meant Pasha could fulfil another ambition. 'I have always wanted to be on *Strictly*, and London is a city I've always dreamed of living in,' he reveals. 'So I guess it's a good thing they come together as a package.'

As an all-rounder, Pasha says that every dance means something different to him.

'Each dance is special to me because it has its own character and its own flavour, which you cannot take away and put into any other dance,' he explains. 'It's like a box of chocolates – there are lots of different types of chocolate and you would like to try each and every one of them because altogether they make a complete experience.'

After the incredible success of the last two series, passionate Pasha is hoping that Rachel can take him all the way.

'I didn't think I could top my first year on *Strictly*, but series 10 was even better,' he says. 'I've been in the final two years running. Let's try and make it a hat trick!'

Strictly
THE CARD GAME

Have you ever fancied seeing your favourite *Strictly* stars face each other in a dance-off? With our game you can shuffle the kings, queens and jumping jacks of the dance floor, from the past ten series, and pit their points against each other to win the pack.

HOW TO PLAY

Pop out the cards, shuffle and deal face down to all players. Each player then holds their stack of cards face up, looking only at the top card.

The player to the left of the dealer starts by choosing a category (e.g. Best ballroom score) and stating its value. The other players then read out the value of the same category from their own card and the highest – or lowest in the case of low score – wins, taking all the other cards from the round and adding them to the bottom of their own pile.

If two or more values are the same as the speaker's card, the cards go into the centre pot and are added to the next win. The winner of the previous round begins as the speaker in the next round. The overall winner is the person left with all the cards.

ALL MARKS ARE OUT OF A POSSIBLE 40

Highest wins in every category EXCEPT 'Low Score', when the smallest number takes the cards.

PUZZLE SOLUTIONS

Crossword

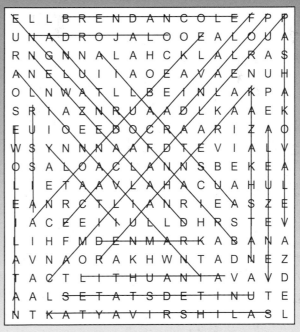

```
M  J     L  K  Z        H
HAUER    OLA JORDAN    AN
T  S     G  T  E       R R
TESSDALY    N  A    FERN
B  I     N  A       I  Y
JAMES              TOM
K                  N  P
LEWIS              HAYES
R  A               P  N
   ANN             HARDY
G  W     M     G   L  L
KARA     LISARILEY
V  I     C  C  B  O  T
VICTORIA    A  B  UNTON
N  E     Y  Y  B  A  N
```

Word Search

```
E L L B R E N D A N C O L E F P P
U N A D R O J A L O O E A L O U A
R N G N N A L A H C K L A L R A S
A N E L U I T A O E A V A E N U H
O L N W A T L L B E I N L A K P A
S R I A Z N R U A A D L K A A E K
E U I O E E D O C R A A R I Z A O
W S Y N N N A A F D T E V I A L V
O S A L O A C L A N N S B E K E A
L I E T A A V L A H A C U A H U L
E A N R C T L I A N R I E A S Z E
I A C E E I K U L L D H R S T E V
L I H F M D E N M A R K A B A N A
A V N A O R A K H W N T A D N E Z
T A C T L I T H U A N I A V A V D
A A L S E T A T S D E T I N U T E
N T K A T Y A V I R S H I L A S L
```

Aliona = Kazakhstan
Anton = England
Brendan = New Zealand
Brian = United States
Camilla = Denmark
Flavia = Italy

Karen = Venezuela
Katya = Lithuania
Natalie = Australia
Ola = Poland
Pasha = Russia

BEHIND THE JUDGES' TABLE

It's the best seat in the house with an incredible view of the dance floor, but there's only room for four. Let us take you behind the judges' desk so you can imagine what it's like to be in their sparkly shoes.

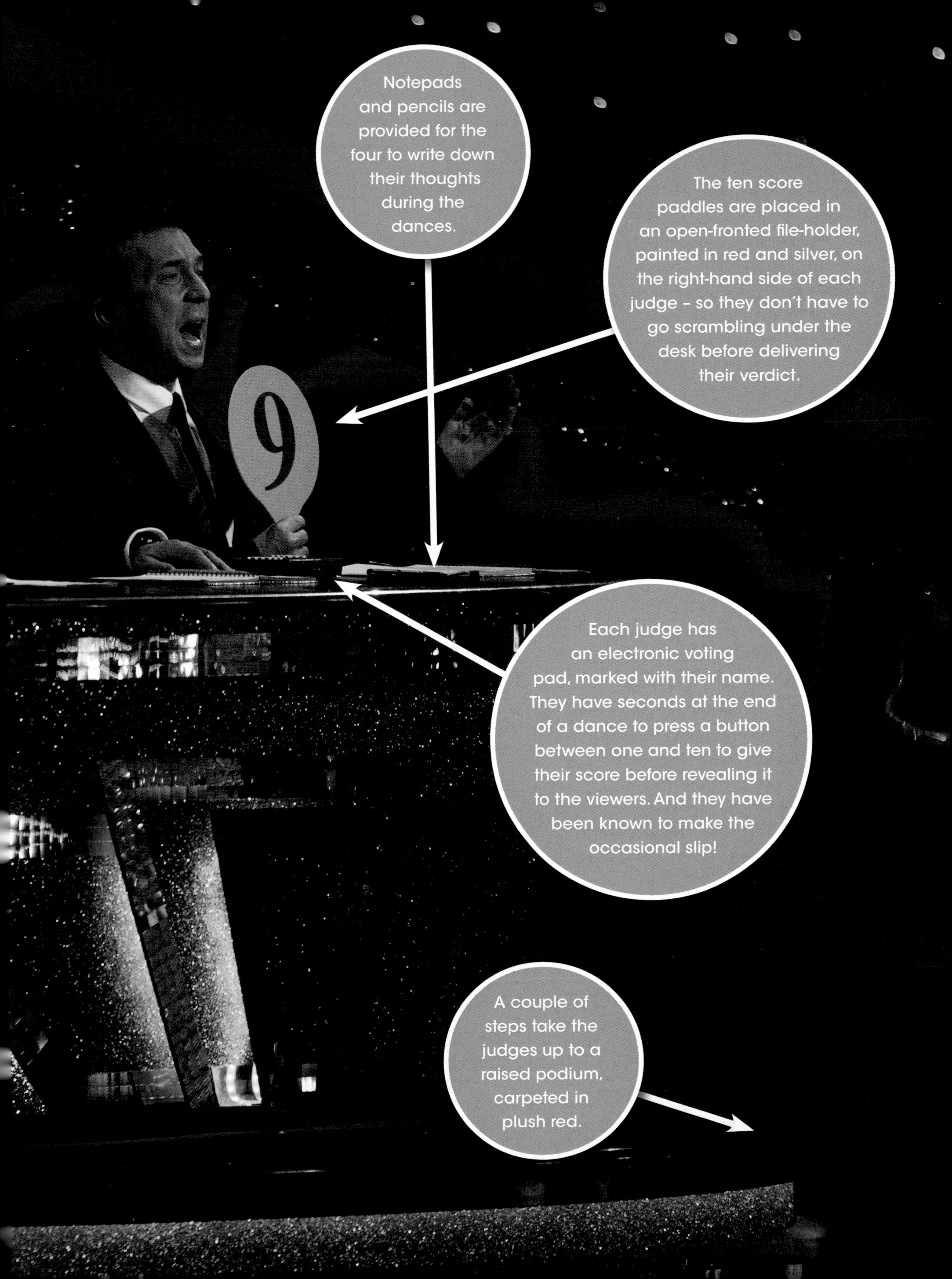
Notepads and pencils are provided for the four to write down their thoughts during the dances.
The ten score paddles are placed in an open-fronted file-holder, painted in red and silver, on the right-hand side of each judge – so they don't have to go scrambling under the desk before delivering their verdict.
9
Each judge has an electronic voting pad, marked with their name. They have seconds at the end of a dance to press a button between one and ten to give their score before revealing it to the viewers. And they have been known to make the occasional slip!
A couple of steps take the judges up to a raised podium, carpeted in plush red.

Tony JACKLIN

The golfing legend is keen to practise a new kind of swing. 'I love music and I do think I've got a sense of rhythm,' he says. 'I just want to get stuck into it. I'm looking forward to dancing with Aliona very much.

'I'm entering with an open mind and I think I'm a quick learner, but she'll have to be a little bit patient with me at the start. My memory's not that good, so remembering all these moves is not that easy for me.'

But the Ryder Cup legend is worried that his partner will think his footwork is below par. 'I'm not sure my dancing prowess is up to much at this point – but Aliona is doing her best to whip me into shape!'

Tony, 69, is the most successful British golfer of all time, having triumphed at a multitude of tournaments including the PGA Tour, European Tour and Senior Tour. He was Ryder Cup captain four times and is credited with changing European fortunes in the tournament, taking the team to its first victory in 28 years in 1985. His name hangs in the World Golf Hall of Fame and in 1990 he was awarded a CBE. Since retiring from golf, he has lived in Florida and concentrated on designing courses around the world. He is also patron of the English Deaf Golf Association, having suffered hearing impairment for 25 years.

The fact that he lives so far from his native England is one of the reasons he decided to take part in the show.

'I've been living in Florida for 20 years and I think a few people have forgotten who I am and what I did,' he explains. 'I've been spending more time in England in the summer, around the golf tournaments and doing some TV commentary, so when I was offered Strictly I said, "OK, why not." If you don't keep reminding people who you are then they forget. So here I am!'

During initial training, however, Aliona will spend some time in Florida – and Tony was keen to show off his culinary skills.

'I will barbecue for her because I barbecue all the time,' he reveals. 'And I've got an outside fish-and-chip cooker, where I do the best fish and chips in Florida. No messing.'

Aliona
VILANI

Last year, Aliona missed out on the show after fracturing her ankle in training, and Iveta Lukosiute was drafted in to partner Johnny Ball. This year the tables were turned when the Russian redhead, who had intended to call it quits, stepped in to replace injured dancer Natalie Lowe.

'Natalie has a fractured foot and she needs to rest until it gets better,' explains Aliona. 'It's very strange. It's exactly what happened to me, but you never know what is going to happen and I'm happy to come back on the show.'

Aliona trained at a school for classical ballet and performing arts in Russia and began her dancing career at the age of 11, when she began competing in ballroom competitions. Two years later she won a scholarship at the Kaiser Dance Academy in New York, where she learned salsa, hip hop and jazz. In 2000, she became a US National Youth Champion in Ten Dance, where dancers compete in classic ballroom and Latin dances, and at 17 she became the youngest professional dancer in the US.

As well as teaching, performing and competing, Aliona continued her studies, achieving an Excellence Diploma in Visual Arts and Fashion Design. She joined *Strictly* in series 7, dancing with Rav Wilding, and made it to the final the following year with Matt Baker. The talented pair were pipped at the post by Kara Tointon but she made up for it in series 9, picking up the glitterball with McFly drummer Harry Judd.

Despite her success in the show, she insists personality is more important than talent when it comes to her celebrity.

'For me it's not about getting someone good, it's about getting someone I can get on with,' she says. 'It's the most important thing because we are going to be spending so much time together. If they are a brilliant dancer, or have the potential to be a great dancer, but we don't get on, it's not going to work because you have to spend all day, every day together and that's stressful.'

Having partnered Matt and Harry, she believes it's a competitive nature that gives a contestant the edge.

'Something has to drive you. It's all good fun, and you don't have to be competitive, but after a couple of weeks when it really starts to mean something to you, you cherish it more, and you want to give it your all, so competitiveness really helps.'

DARCEY

The UK's most famous ballerina, Darcey Bussell, added a touch of grace and beauty to the judging panel, but she admits she was jittery about her new role.

'I was extremely nervous,' she reveals. 'It took me a good month to relax. You think you know the show incredibly well, and I had been a guest judge, but it's very different when you're there full time.'

Luckily, fellow judges Len, Craig and Bruno welcomed the new girl with open arms.

'The guys were great,' she says. 'I asked a lot of questions and they were always there to answer them for me. I wasn't expecting to get so much feedback from them, because they are all busy people, but they always had time for me and that helped me settle in quickly.

'They let me feel that I had a role, which was important, so I didn't feel I was stepping on any toes.'

Once she'd shaken her initial nerves, though, Darcey had a ball.

'I absolutely loved it. To me it was like being in a company again because, when you're a dancer, you are used to being in a group where you're all passionate about one thing. It's what I missed most when I retired from ballet and now I have that again with *Strictly*. I feel very fortunate.'

Was Louis a worthy winner?

The three finalists were all amazing but, for me, Louis always had that edge. As a gymnast he already had strength and flexibility but when he found that flair, and confidence, he had it all. Their extraordinary showdance clinched it. Flavia really captured his strengths and delivered that 'wow' factor.

What did you make of the final?

All three of the last couples could easily have won so it was very exciting. The showdances were incredible, although Kimberley's Beyoncé number was a bit wild! Denise and James pulled out every trick in the book with lift after lift, and it was stunning.

Who was the biggest surprise?

Dani Harmer. She really used what she had to her advantage, and ended up emerging as the thinking dancer, taking in everything Vincent told her and working hard. So when she came out she was dynamite.

Who improved the most?

Michael Vaughan. He had real problems at the start but he put in the hours and did amazingly well. It's tough for a sportsman because they start without either the performance or dance experience, so he should be incredibly proud of what he achieved.

Favourite dance of the series?

There were so many memorable ones but Denise and James's Charleston at Wembley sticks out. It was flawless, really impressive and so professionally danced. Another was Kimberley's tango. She had a beautiful neck and shoulders, and she played it with such attack. The pout sold it.

Jerry Hall's poise and elegance weren't quite enough to keep her in.

Who do you wish had stayed longer?

I would like to have seen Jerry Hall make it further. She's used to the public gaze on her and she has that grace and elegance, but she didn't really have the drive.

Favourite moments as a judge?

Dancing behind the desk. I'm not very good at sitting still so any time I could get up and have a little boogie – usually with Craig – relieved the pressure a bit.

Looking forward to the next series?

Definitely. And, fingers crossed, I won't be as nervous this time. To be in a second series, with the show being in its tenth year, is fabulous. It's the best show to be on!

Michael Vaughan 'put in the hours' and improved the most.

Dani gives a Venetian twist to her Viennese waltz in week 9.

Abbey CLANCY

As a model, Abbey has her fair share of glamour in her everyday life. But she is still looking forward to being 'Strictlified' every Saturday night.

'I think the costume designer Vicky Gill is sensational,' she says. 'She knew beforehand who was in the show and she's tried to tailor the outfits to everyone's personal style, but with millions of diamonds and feathers and all kinds on them. I absolutely love them!'

It's not the first time the 27-year-old Liverpudlian has been through a TV talent show, as she got her big break as one of the 13 finalists in the 2006 series *Britain's Next Top Model*. After coming second she became a catwalk sensation and modelled for numerous magazines, ranking in *FHM* magazine's annual 100 Sexiest Women in the World.

Now married to Stoke City striker Peter Crouch, with a two-year-old daughter, she says she will limit her practice sessions to partner Aljaž Skorjanec and won't be trying out her moves at home.

'Pete does like to dance but I probably won't practise with him because I think it'll just confuse me,' she says. 'I'll just stick to Aljaž. I need to get used to his height. Aljaž's partner Janette had a pic with Pete before and she was up to his belt!'

Despite her superslim figure, Abbey doesn't work out and says her fitness levels are 'horrendous'. With training eight to ten hours a day, she admits she is a little worried she will lose weight.

'I've been trying to eat a lot more the past few weeks because I don't want to shrink,' she reveals. 'I eat loads anyway. There's a myth that I starve myself, but I eat what I want, I've got a healthy appetite. With the training you're naturally more hungry. Everyone is just constantly eating on the show because you burn so much energy, so you need fuel otherwise you just can't function and you get tired and feel a bit sick.'

Although determined to learn a new skill and have fun along the way, Abbey feels she lacks the competitive edge.

'I'm the least competitive person there is,' she says. 'I'm the eldest of four, so I've grown up letting the babies win every game. Obviously I'd like to do well for myself and I'd like my daughter and family to be proud, but I wouldn't say I'm going to kick everyone's behind!'

Aljaž SKORJANEC

Aljaž was over the moon when he found out he and girlfriend Janette Manrara were both joining the *Strictly* line-up.

'That was my biggest wish because we always try to look for work that will keep us together,' he admits. '*Strictly* is such a great opportunity for individual dancers, so it wouldn't matter if one of us didn't get in as the other would still have done it. But both of us being chosen means we feel really blessed.'

The call for the show came when Aljaž was in London, grabbing a few groceries in the local shop. 'We had the interviews, so we were all very excited but anxious,' he recalls. 'I was about to go home from the shop, and I got the call saying I'd been accepted and I dropped the bags in shock! I couldn't believe what I'd just heard.'

The superfit Slovenian slipped on his first dancing shoes at the age of five in a kindergarten group. A year later he won his first competition and by seven he was a national champ. Together with dance partner Valerija Rahle, he bagged a total of 19 Slovenian championships, in ballroom, Latin and Ten Dance, a challenging combination of ten ballroom and Latin dances, before he turned professional.

In 2010, he joined the world tour of *Burn the Floor*, which is where he met Janette, and the show provided the perfect training ground for *Strictly.*

As a Ten dancer, Aljaž is a great all-rounder but his favourite dances are the paso doble and the foxtrot. 'I love the passion of the paso and the frame because it's quite similar to the one in ballroom, very linear. The foxtrot appeals to me because there is no closing action, we never close the feet, so it's very fluid and very calm.'

At 23, the talented dancer will be the baby of the bunch – and it sound like he could be the sweetest when it comes to teaching his celebrity partner. No cracking the whip or throwing a strop for him.

'I always want to make sure my partner is having a good time and enjoying herself,' he says. 'That's my first priority and then, of course, teaching her how to dance. But I want to do that in the nicest possible way so that she never feels like I'm pressuring her or putting too much on her shoulders.'

Russell Grant

STATS MAN

The former series 9 favourite has been beavering away in the archives to bring you the *Strictly* stats. So here are some dance numbers with a difference …

★ THE CELEBS

A total of **132** celebrities have taken part in ten series. Their professions are:

45 actors
28 broadcasters/presenters
26 sports stars
14 musicians
5 comedians
6 models
2 MPs
2 chefs
1 magician
1 gardener
1 astrologer – he was very good!
1 Nancy Dell'Olio

★ PROFESSIONS THAT HAVE MADE IT TO THE TOP THREE

10 actors
7 musicians
5 presenters/broadcasters
6 sport stars
1 comedian
1 model

★ WINNERS

Louis's win puts sports stars neck and neck with actors when it comes to winning.
3 actors: Jill Halfpenny, Tom Chambers, Kara Tointon
3 sport stars: Darren Gough, Mark Ramprakash and Louis Smith
2 presenters: Natasha Kaplinsky and Chris Hollins
2 musicians: Alesha Dixon and Harry Judd

At **23**, Louis is the youngest winner. The oldest is Chris Hollins at **38**. So far five winners have been in their thirties and five in their twenties.

★ SUPER SCORERS

Highest average score over a series:

Alesha Dixon: **36.5**

Ricky Whittle: **35.9**

Rachel Stevens: **35.8**

Kara Tointon: **35.7**

Harry Judd: **35.6**

★ MOST GENEROUS JUDGE

In her stint as full-time judge for one series, plus three shows in series 7, Darcey has raised her 10 paddle almost as often as Craig has managed in all ten series. Bruno is by far the most generous over the decade.

Darcey: **23**

Craig: **30**

Len: **88**

Bruno: **113**

★ TENS PER SERIES

Those standards just keep getting better – and the number of 10s awarded by the judges keeps creeping up. With only one awarded in the first series, things have certainly improved.

Series 1: **1**

Series 2: **7**

Series 3: **13**

Series 4: **14**

Series 5: **37**

Series 6: **59**

Series 7: **46**

Series 8: **51**

Series 9: **57**

Series 10: **59**

★ TOP TENS

Top of the leader board for the number of 10s earned in a series are two amazing dancers who still missed out on the glitterball.

1. Ricky Whittle, series 7: **28**

2. Rachel Stevens, series 6: **25**

3. Harry Judd, series 9: **22**

4. Lisa Snowdon, series 6: **20**

4. Kara Tointon, series 8: **20**

4. Denise Van Outen, series 10: **20**

4. Kimberley Walsh, series 10: **20**

★ THE GRAND TOTAL

There have **1,031** competitive dances performed over the ten series of *Strictly*.

★ PERFECT TENS

A perfect score has been awarded on **26** occasions. A whopping **344** individual scores of **10** have been awarded.

★ MOST- AND LEAST- PERFORMED DANCE

The dance that has been performed competitively the most times on the show is the cha-cha-cha with a whopping **99** performances. Least performed are the rock and roll and Lindy Hop, both performed **twice** in series 7.

★ WEMBLEY

The dance floor is made up of **1,000** separate pieces and measures **35**m x **20**m. That's nearly **six** times the size of the normal floor – that's a lot of ground to cover!

There are **350** moving lights and **300** static lights, with **20**km of cables for them.

The audience number close to **6,000**.

★ MUSIC MAESTROS

Frank Sinatra is the artist most likely to be chosen for a routine. His songs have been performed by the band **27** times.

Michael Bublé is second in the charts with **18** numbers and Robbie Williams has been danced to **17** times.

Sinatra is an Anton Du Beke favourite – he's danced to Ol' Blue Eyes **five** times.

On Saturday night on average there are about **50** instruments in the orchestra.

The band get through about **8–10** guitar strings a week, which over a whole series of *Strictly* amounts to about **4.5** miles.

The band play live to an audience of about **11** million viewers each week – which would fill the O2 Arena **600** times over.

★ THE MAKEOVER STATS

Over the first nine series the hair and make-up team got through the following:

108 litres of liquid glitter

315 mascara sticks

360 full heads of hair extensions

720 bottles of nail varnish

1,764 sets of fake eyelashes

4,536 cans of hairspray

6,300 tissues

33,390 hair pins

Figures courtesy of the *It Takes Two* BBC Production Team, 2012

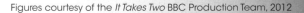

Ben COHEN

Rugby ace Ben is keen to tackle the dances with his partner Kristina Rihanoff, but he's leaving the rugby at the rehearsal-room door.

'I will bring a work ethic, but I'm not as competitive as I used to be,' he explains. 'I've spent 20 years with that bit between my teeth, getting up and growling at other people all day, and I'm past that now. I'm going to enjoy the show and embrace it.

'I'm going into the unknown and it's hard to be competitive about the unknown, so I'll enjoy it week by week. I'll put the hours in, I'll work hard. I train every day anyway so it's going to be the same sort of thing for me.'

The sporting hero is the tenth-highest points scorer in the history of English rugby and was part of the team that won the World Cup in Australia in 2003.

Born in Northampton, he began his professional career at 17 and played for Northampton Saints, French side Brive and Sale Sharks. In 2011 he retired from the sport to run his charitable foundation, which aims to combat bullying and homophobia.

Ben follows in the footsteps of rugby hunks Matt Dawson and Austin Healey, and says they've already been in touch to give him some words of advice.

'I haven't had any stick from my rugby pals but I've had Austin and Matt on the phone,' he reveals. 'Matt set the bar and, fair play, he was really good. I was watching him on YouTube the other day and I dropped him a message saying, "You were bloody good." I've got a lot of work to do.'

The beefy 34 year old promises he will bring the guns out a few weeks into the series. 'I think the buttons are going to get lower and lower, and the shirt may come off,' he laughs. 'I think it's going to happen, right. I haven't had a spray tan yet, but no doubt I will. I'll embrace it all, and that's what it's about.'

Kristina RIHANOFF

Partnering former Bond star Colin Salmon last year. Kristina left earlier than many, including the pair themselves, would have liked. But the tall, elegant actor did tower over the tiny dancer.

'Colin is a great character and it was a pleasure getting to know him on the show,' she explains. 'But series 10 was the most challenging for me as a professional. My partner was 1 foot 2 inches taller than me, which was definitely a challenge. But I'm proud that we did our best and had a lot of fun along the way.'

The sexy Siberian began studying ballet at six and went on to train in Latin and standard ballroom, entering her first competition at seven, winning numerous youth competitions in her Russian region. At 16, she turned to teaching, while still attending college, where she earned a master's degree in Tourism and Hospitality.

In 2001, Kristina was asked to the States to compete professionally and moved to Seattle where she studied new styles including salsa, American rhythm and exhibition dances. With partner Michael Wentink, Kristina began to specialise in Latin, winning the South African Championship and reaching the semi-finals of the 2007 British Open in Blackpool.

During *Strictly*, Kristina has had a mixed bag of dance partners – from the hilarious John Sergeant to the hard-working and talented Jason Donovan. But the blonde beauty believes there is a way to teach everyone, even those with two left feet.

'The main thing is to understand the other person's way of learning,' she says. 'I have been teaching a lot of beginners, and you need to find a way to make it simple for them while having fun and finding cool ways to explain things.

'Then, even when the work gets hard, they still feel like they are having a good time and accomplishing something great. Respect, of course, is also the key to a successful working relationship, no matter what.'

COSTUMES

In the midst of a hectic final day, as the finalists get the finishing touches to their make-up and production staff bustle busily around the corridors, in contrast, the costume department is an oasis of calm. Costume designer **VICKY GILL** (above), who is usually swamped by last-minute alterations, is for once enjoying the lull – somewhat nervously.

'It's really quite calm, which is unusual,' she says. 'But everybody has worked really hard this week – late nights and lots of midweek fittings – so that today wouldn't be too horrendous. The dress run went really well, but I don't know if that's a good thing. I'd rather have hitches in the dress run than for things to go wrong when we go live.'

Vicky's colleague Michelle Wells is taking care of the one last-minute alteration of the day – sticking tiny stones on to Louis Smith's blue-and-white leggings for the spectacular show dance to come.

'Originally, because of all their lifts, Louis and Flavia requested that they had no crystals, which is a bit too dull for *Strictly*,' explains Vicky. 'So we pleaded with him to have a few sparkles put on.'

Michelle dabs tiny blobs of glue on the hips and down the side of the leggings, then painstakingly adds each tiny stone, one by one. As she works Vicky and designer Nicola Atkinson discuss the look and have a change of heart, telling Michelle to wipe the glue from the white areas. 'The white looks so clean,' says Vicky. 'We put silver on Flav's, but I think the white works best on here.'

Looking around the neat, orderly room, with stark whitewashed walls, it seems a world away from the glitz and glamour of *Strictly*'s unforgettable outfits. White plastic boxes, marked 'belts', 'cufflinks', 'shoe brushes' and

Louis and Flavia take to the floor in their newly sparkly outfits.

It's a bling thing: Michelle adds some stones to Louis's show-dance leggings.

'white collars' line the walls and the corridor just outside the costume department, but there is very little sparkle on show – with the exception of a skimpy little number, designed for Kimberley Walsh. The silver-blue fringed Latin outfit features cutaway panels at the waist and hips, which look sensational on the slim Girls Aloud star.

'That really is a great look for Kimberley, because you can see how small her waist is,' says the designer. 'At the same time, we couldn't put Kimberley in a flapper dress for the Charleston because she's so tiny at the waist and very curvaceous – meaning a straight-down dress like that would only hide her beautiful shape.

The professionals take to floor with ties intact – with some notable exceptions.

'With Dani, who is very petite, you can't just put a ballroom dress on her every week – she'd look silly – so she's had lots of different looks. Everybody is individual, with different shapes; so you need different concepts.'

For the costume department, the hard work begins before the launch show, when the celebrities come for their first fittings, and Vicky begins to build up an idea of the styles and shapes that work. Part of her job is to add a little extra confidence to each performance – but she has to tread carefully.

'When people join *Strictly* each and every one of them – although they've never said it – are incredibly afraid of costume.

'At the end, they tend to show more flesh but to start with I have a little list of things that people don't want to show. It doesn't matter how slim someone is, or how big, we all have our insecurities. We spend a lot of time with them, we build a mannequin to their exact shape prior to the run, and there's a lot of preparation.'

Despite the meticulous planning, ideas are often altered in the run-up to the Saturday-night broadcast. 'During the week the lighting, projection, costumes, make-up and hair are off doing their own thing, and we only come together on Friday and Saturday so sometimes it doesn't work. For example, one week Dani had some black painted on her eyes, which, in isolation, looked very nice but wasn't quite right with the rest of the look. In the run-up to the show everybody is reassessing everything, and details get changed. So we might be taking off ties, adding braces, changing shoes and tweaking.'

With an hour or so to go before the live final, discussions are still under way about which ties the professional dancers will wear in the group number, and a vest top is requested for Louis, who will be dancing his final routine topless and will need to cover up when he's off the floor. Vicky and the team remain unflappable. 'One week we had to tack Erin's skirt on to her, because we didn't have time to machine

VICKY'S PICK

'My favourite dress of the series was Denise Van Outen's quarter-final jive-fusion dress. Because she'd already done the jive to "Tutti Frutti", we couldn't have another dress in the same vein. But they started in a jazz-bar setting, on an evening out, so it was a bit more stylish. I loved the red-and-gold colour combination, the silhouette really suited her, and it looked fresh and modern. It could translate into a fashion garment.'

it,' she recalls. 'We just had to hope Richard didn't pull it off in the dance. On Halloween, we cut the hem on Kimberley's paso dress to an arc about a minute before she went on, so she didn't get her heel caught.'

The toughest week for wardrobe, says Vicky, is Wembley, when the whole show has to be packed up and shipped to the north-London arena. 'There are 14 extra dancers, with the backing dancers, and 98 costumes,' she says. 'They start rehearsals on Thursday, and everything has to be as ready as possible on Wednesday and transported to the arena; so it is certainly the busiest week.

'It's unrealistic but somehow, with a little bit of compromise and a few chats, we get there. The show is going to happen, no matter what, so it's got to be done. We haven't had naked people yet – half-naked, yes, but not naked!'

Family favourite: Denise in the red-and-gold dress for the jive–quickstep fusion.

Fiona FULLERTON

The Nigerian-born actress is a huge *Strictly* fan, and spends many of her Saturday nights watching the show with her whole family. Now she's thrilled to be stepping out on to the hallowed dance floor.

'I was looking for a challenge and an adventure, and swapping my wellington boots from living in the country for a whole load of sequins is very appealing,' she admits. 'It is every girl's dream, to be dressed up and pampered and to learn how to dance.'

The 56 year old is best known for her starring role alongside Roger Moore – as KGB spy Pola Ivanova in the 1985 Bond film *A View to a Kill*. Her 30-year career has seen her star on stage and TV as well as in movies, and she is now a writer and property-investment guru.

As an avid viewer, Fiona admires many of the former contestants but her *Strictly* hero is series 8 winner, Kara Tointon.

'I absolutely loved Kara,' she says. 'I thought she was wonderful. She had such grace and was really the epitome of *Strictly*. I think she was probably one of the loveliest contestants they have had on the show.'

As an aficionado of the show, the elegant star is prepared to go for the sexy Latin numbers but says she is a little more wary of the sedate foxtrot.

'That's the dance that scares me most,' she admits. 'Every year I see this show and I've watched it from the beginning, and it always seems to be the one that unravels the most contestants.'

If anyone can guide her through the classic dance, it's ballroom-king Anton du Beke and she's thrilled to have landed him as her pro.

'I'm very, very, very happy,' she says. 'We did a lot of interviews leading up to the launch show and in all the interviews I've done, I've said, "I want Anton."

'Anton is an exquisite dancer. He's also lovely with the ladies; he's a gentleman and I think I will learn well from him. And he has a great sense of humour.'

But which 007 would the former Bond girl most like to take to the floor with?

'Pierce Brosnan,' she says. 'There's something lovely about him, and suave. Or Anton Du Bond!'

Anton DU BEKE

As the show celebrates its tenth year, Anton returns as one of only two original dancers – the other being Brendan Cole. As the godfather of *Strictly*, he feels it just gets better and better.

'I think the standard has improved every year,' he observes. 'The professionals do more with their partners than we used to do, and demand more from their partners. Then there are the props and backdrops, better production. The whole thing has really come on over the years.'

Sadly, the ballroom king has yet to reach the final – having been paired with the likes of Ann Widdecombe, Kate Garraway and Nancy Dell'Olio along the way. And last year's celeb, Jerry Hall, didn't make the model pupil either, leaving second after scoring 18 for all three dances.

Anton came late to dancing, joining a class in Kent at 14 after meeting his sister there and seeing it was packed with girls. A keen amateur boxer and football player, he soon found a new passion on the dance floor.

After training in Latin and ballroom for three years he chose to specialise in ballroom. Leaving school at 16, he worked in various jobs to pay for his lessons and danced in the evenings, and, in 1997, he met Erin Boag, who has been his professional partner ever since.

This will be the first *Strictly* he has been without Erin, who joined the first-ever show at his side.

'It won't be the same without Erin,' he admits. 'And I will miss her. But she has done the show for ten years and she decided she didn't want to do it any more. That's her decision and she's happy with it. I spoke to her the other day and she's looking forward to watching the series. She's very excited by the pairings and can now sit back and enjoy the dancing in comfort.'

Julien MACDONALD

Strictly's first fashion designer is set to dazzle on the dance floor – and not necessarily because of his footwork.

'On the day of the launch show, while everyone else was practising, I was in my dressing room putting more crystals on my outfit!' he reveals. 'Everyone said, "You look a bit more sparkly." I told them I had stuck a couple of crystals on it and I've got a can of glitter spray in my bag. I intend to sparkle all the way.'

The Welsh fashion guru started his career working for Karl Lagerfeld and was named British Fashion Designer of the Year in 2001. In the same year he became chief designer at Givenchy, replacing the Alexander McQueen. He now boasts an international client list of A-list stars, including Beyoncé and Selena Gomez and, with a reputation for show-stopping, high-glamour dresses, he is perfect for the glitzy world of *Strictly*. But he may cause wardrobe a bit of a headache.

'So far I've been the *Strictly* fashion judge,' he laughs. 'All the girls and the guys come to me and say, "Julien, what do you think of my dress?" I say, "Oh, Deborah, go and ask them to make it shorter and cut off that sleeve!" Then wardrobe come to me and say, "Julien, you are telling everyone to change their outfit" and I say, "What? I didn't say anything!"'

Julien is paired with new dancer Janette Manrara – and is not letting her out of his sight.

'Janette's going to be moving into my house during the show,' he jokes. 'She's not leaving. We're gonna be dancing around the kitchen!'

As a judge himself – on *Britain & Ireland's Next Top Model* – the 42-year-old fashionista won't be taking any flack from the judges.

'I watch the show and I never get why all the celebs stand there and just take a grilling from the judges,' he says.

'At the end of the day I don't mind when someone gives you constructive criticism, but if they dish it out, they should be able to take it too. I am definitely going to answer them back. I'm not afraid of the Revel Horwood!'

Janette MANRARA

Janette will have plenty of moral support when she joins the *Strictly* company. Not only is she already friends with a lot of the professionals but her boyfriend, Aljaž, is also a new dancer on the show.

'Having him with me is amazing. It's great that we both got the call together and I'm so excited to have him by my side. He'll help me whenever I'm stressing and pulling my hair out.'

'I'm nervous about joining because it's such a massive show, but I'm also ecstatic because I've got amazing friends there, so it's going to be a really interesting, fun time.'

Originally trained in musical theatre, Janette starred in TV shows as a child and came to ballroom late, starting her formal dance training at 19 while studying finance at college. 'The dance studio I was going to closed down and my teacher Manuel Castro and his wife Lory set up their own school. Manuel encouraged me to pursue a professional career but I thought he was crazy. There was no way I could compete against people who had been training since they were five, but it worked out well.'

Her career took off when she made the final eight in series 5 of *So You Think You Can Dance?* in the US – but she almost didn't audition at all.

'I had auditioned the season before. I got to the top 30 then I was told "no",' she recalls. 'So I wasn't going to try out, but my dance teacher persuaded me and I was the first one they said "yes" to. It was a completely different experience. The whole journey was magnificent and it made me realise that I can achieve anything I set my mind to. I owe my entire dance career to the show. If it weren't for that I would have been working in a bank.'

Janette's real passion for ballroom and Latin was ignited when she joined *Burn the Floor*, under the tutelage of Jason Gilkison, *Strictly*'s latest head of choreography, and his dance partner Peta Roby.

'I've always liked ballroom and Latin, but I fell in love with it then,' she says. 'I just love the connection. I love the intimacy of it.'

It was at an audition for the show in London's West End that she met Aljaž, and they have been together for three years. But how will she feel if he waltzes off with the trophy? 'It's direct competition,' she says. 'I'll be happy for him, but I'll secretly wish it could have been me!'

HAIR

Down a long corridor from the make-up room, stylist **NEALE PIRIE** (below) is creating the striking coiffures to complete the *Strictly* look. For Neale, the quick change during the final show means each of the leading ladies needs four styles, which can adapt easily from one to the next.

For example, for this year's final Dani Harmer – who is being teased and tousled by Neale as we speak – starts off with two ponytails hidden under a fake bun for her tango, and in the break, the bun comes off, the ponytails are pulled up and the front pulled back to create a Mohawk. For the third dance – which she never got to perform – a pink ponytail extension is due to be attached. 'The first dance that everyone is doing they have done before so we know that look well,' says Neale. 'But it's transferring that into the new look, which we haven't done yet, and that can prove difficult.'

Like Lisa Armstrong (see page 102), Neale starts planning the look during the week, but he doesn't have long to decide on the many styles. 'We wait for the dress designs then Lisa will have an idea of what she wants, the dancers may have a bit of an idea of what they want, so we piece it together like that. The celebs are in on the discussion but we know what the dance is going to do to the hairstyle and how the look works together. What looks nice with long hair might not dance well with long hair, so it could get screwed up.'

The talented stylist cut his teeth in the theatre and says the skills he learnt there come in handy on *Strictly*. 'We often base styles on movies and also in the theatre we're used to doing quick changes so that really helps,' he says. 'And we do definitely have our theatrical moments.'

Vincent gets the '50s vibe as his quiff (below) is put in.

The hair department is a mêlée of blasting hairdryers and noisy chatter. A dummy head in the corner has a wig with a massive quiff for Vincent's final jive. ('We'll probably get that on Craig at some point,' quips Neale.) A full staff of five hairdressers and three assistants have been drafted in to deal with the heavy workload. And it's not just the finalists that they are styling. 'We have all the original couples – so 28 in total,' he explains. 'The pro girls are having two different looks. The returning celebrities are just having one look and all the others are having four. I don't know how we do it!'

Opposite: Neale Pirie and his team of stylists get the dancers ready for the final.

Dani is prepped for the first of her big numbers, the tango.

Natalie GUMEDE

The former *Coronation Street* star was last seen heading to jail after a hard-hitting storyline. But Natalie hopes *Strictly* will help her to put the spectre of the evil Kirsty way behind her.

'Kirsty was a very difficult, troubled, dark character, and I can't protest enough the difference between myself and her,' she says. 'I'm sure by the end of the first show, when the viewers see how "Strictlified" I've been, they'll see we're nothing alike and they'll close the door on that for sure.'

During her 18-month stint in *Corrie*, the Burnley-born actress won Best Newcomer at the British Soap Awards in 2012 and Villain of the Year in 2013. An avid *Strictly* fan she says her appearance on the show will come as no surprise to her former soap-star colleagues.

'They know how much I love the show,' she smiles. 'I was talking about it all last year, so they'll probably have a little laugh to themselves.'

Natalie's first TV appearance came at the age of 11, when she was picked to present the north-west regional broadcast for BBC's *Children in Need*. After a three-year course studying acting and musical theatre at the Italia Conti school in London, she landed roles in *Waterloo Road, The Persuasionists* and *Ideal* before joining the cast of *Corrie* in 2011.

As well as dancing with *Strictly* champ Artem Chigvintsev, the stunning 29 year old is looking forward to gaining a touch of Saturday-night sparkle for the show.

'It's a wild experience because you'll never look like this in another job or any platform anywhere,' she says. 'It's really strange to look in the mirror and keep seeing this completely different person looking back at you. We take all day getting ready. We go in and out, more make-up, more hair, back on a merry-go-round until your inner ballroom diva is unleashed!'

Natalie admits she's 'far too terrified' to have come up with any clever tactics for the show, but is ready to work hard – which will be music to Artem's ears.

'I just want to enjoy it. I want to try as hard as I can, do as many weeks as I can and just enjoy every minute. I want to soak up every aspect of it, because I really feel like I'm living a dream and getting the opportunity to express something in myself that hasn't yet been expressed.'

Artem CHIGVINTSEV

In his first year on *Strictly* he twirled Kara Tointon to victory. He followed that by reaching the semi-finals with Holly Valance. Last year, he and partner Fern Britton only made it to week 6 – but Artem has no complaints.

'Fern was lovely and was such a pleasure to work with,' he reveals. 'She always brought a smile to the training room – even when I cracked the whip! We managed to get to week 6 and then got to dance together on the *Strictly* tour, which was fun.'

The reeling Russian was taken to dance classes by his parents at a young age, as his mother was a big fan of dancing and wanted him to have an interest that would keep him off the streets. He took to it immediately and, when he found himself raking in the competition trophies, he decided he might be good enough to make a career of it.

At 15, he swapped foxtrotting for globe-trotting, leaving Russia to train in Germany, Italy and London before settling in Los Angeles. After reaching the final of *So You Think You Can Dance* in the US, Artem starred in *Burn the Floor* on Broadway and in the West End. He also took a few acting roles – including a part in the US teen soap, *The O.C.*

Going into his fourth series of *Strictly*, the hunky Russian says that he makes sure his celebrity isn't stretched over and above her ability but, in the training room, he's the boss.

'When you first see a contestant you ask them what they're comfortable with, and you have to consider that they're doing something they've never done before. and try to stay in their comfort zone,' he says. 'But the ideas, the music choices and choreography come from us. You expect to tell them what to do and that's what they expect from you. And if they do it right, it's great.'

Keen to be the first dancer in the history of the series to land trophy number two, Artem is raring to go.

'I love working on *Strictly* and my three years on the show have been a blast,' he says. 'Bring on series 11!'

MAKE-UP

The hectic whirl of last-minute rehearsals and technical run-throughs on the day of the *Strictly* final means little free time for the finalists and professionals. One of the few moments of respite is when they sink into a comfortable chair and let hair and make-up designer **LISA ARMSTRONG** (above) and her team work their magic while they relax and swap gossip.

For Lisa, there is no rest on the day. From 10 a.m., she's on her feet, adding some *Strictly* sparkle to a stream of well-known faces for the ultimate live show of the series.

'The final is one of the busiest shows because not only do we have all the celebrities back that we've lost through the weeks, but also we have two or three dances for each remaining couple,' she explains. 'So that's quick hair and make-up changes, which we try out in the dress run, then re-create for the live show. In total, that's eight looks for each finalist.'

The walls of the bustling room are dotted with bulb-lined mirrors and the seven-strong team are surrounded by a bewildering array of products, the tricks of the trade. The dressing tables are heaving with boxes of different foundation shades and more and palettes of eyeshadow in every conceivable hue. Make-up bags stuffed with hundreds of eye pencils and mascaras are piled up on the side, and brushes are laid out in front of each girl, as she creates a work of art, layer by layer, on each new canvas. As well as the make-up there are boxes of false eyelashes and an amazing variety of nail vanish.

'As the series goes on you get to know what you prefer on each person, but we swap around – because I'll do a smoky eye differently to how one of the other girls would – and it's good to get that variety. You work out with each other, with the team and the girls, which products work best. But I don't take notes. It's all up in my head. After the final it all goes to mush!'

Although the make-up is one of the last things to happen on the day, Lisa is perfecting the looks for days beforehand and consulting with hairstylist Neale Pirie and costume designer Vicky Gill. The make-up designs are sketched and added to a folder with the hairstyle and costume design, and each star is given a

Above: Natalie gets a little body shimmer to add to the sparkle. **Below:** Back in the glam camp. Returning celeb Lisa Riley gets a *Strictly* makeover.

slot in the day for their makeover. 'It's all in the planning. People think you turn up with a hairbrush and a lipgloss and off you go, but it has to be planned with precision.'

As the final nears, Lisa moves her box of tricks to the star bar, where the finalists change between dances. With a window of just 10 minutes for a change of costume, hair and make-up, Lisa has no time to create complicated new looks. 'We can't start taking make-up off and reapplying, so you're really adding, building up the look as you go on. We might add a different lip colour, darken the eye or use more of a liner. You can't start with anything too dramatic, because then there's nowhere to go.'

As well as their faces, the make-up team are responsible for the whole body – and not just the fake tan. 'A lot of girls suffer bruises because they're being so active, and sometimes flung about by their partners,' reveals Lisa. 'We have concealer palettes and camouflage palettes, which we also use to cover tattoos. Then we have the shimmer and shine products to make the body glossy.'

The makeovers aren't limited to the ladies either. Craig, Bruno and Len get a smattering of slap, as do the male celebs and professionals. But not all take to it straight away.

'It's all part and parcel of the show and the professionals know that,' she says. 'It's as important as putting on their dance shoes. With the celebrities, if they are performers – like Nicky Byrne or Sid Owen – they're used to having make-up put on, but it's more difficult for the sportsmen because it's so alien to them. But they see the other boys doing it, and they realise it's all part of the show; so they're happy to come in and let us work our magic.'

Opposite: There's no rest for the busy make-up team as the live show draws near.
Below: It's not just a girl thing: Nicky Byrne gets a little touch-up.

ZOE has a BALL

While there's plenty of action and entertainment on the dance floor, *Strictly* viewers who want the story behind the steps and all the gossip from the main show turn to *It Takes Two* which airs five nights a week on BBC2 and is presented by **ZOE BALL**.

Zoe took over from Claudia Winkleman in 2011 and describes the moment she was asked to front the show as an all-time career high. 'I was a fan of the show before I appeared on it in 2005. After that, they could have asked me to sit there every week and sew on the sequins and I would have done it just to get the gossip!'

Zoe danced in the third series of *Strictly* and was partnered with Ian Waite. She was placed third behind Colin Jackson and Darren Gough, who was crowned champion. Zoe received more 10s from the judges in the series than any other competitor – seven in total – though none from Craig! So when she was asked to front *It Takes Two* it seemed like a natural step. But Zoe remembers how nervous she was when she started.

'I was walking onto the set and we thought it was a good idea for me to wear a feather boa. I took a deep breath and inhaled a feather just before my first welcome line. I had to talk through my choking. The show is live and I just had to carry on!'

One of the highlights of Zoe's week is her Wednesday feature with her old dancing partner. 'Ian comes in every week and talks

A tangled web: nobody told Ian Waite that he'd be the only one in fancy dress on the Halloween special.

Mark Ramprakash in 2006, but decided to hang up her sparkly shoes in 2008.

'I remember doing a professional number, and I had two of the gorgeous girls on either side of me, I suddenly thought, it's time to go,' Karen recalls. 'I was the only one of the dancers who is a mum, and it was time for me to bow out. But I left with such a positive feeling and loving the show; so to be invited back to provide a professional dancer's perspective is just wonderful.'

Karen loves the variety of dance talent in the contestants – from dance expert to comic, with the occasional feisty politician thrown in – which means the analysis is never boring.

'I loved Ann Widdecombe,' Karen reveals. 'I queried her heel turns, and she said, "What? What about my heel turns?" She wasn't having any of it.'

Zoe and the team are broadcasting from the Southbank Centre for this year's *It Takes Two* and it's bigger and better than ever. As Zoe says 'I am the luckiest woman in the world – who else has a job where they get to find out all the *Strictly* gossip?'

through how the couples are getting on in training. My favourite bit is where we try out the moves that the couples are trying to do, although he tried to show me a samba move one week and I nearly went flying!

'Ian is pretty game on the show and the production team try to put him in the silliest costumes possible … like last Halloween where he was told everyone else was wearing a costume and turned up as a giant 6-foot spider.'

Another very important part of the *It Takes Two* family is Latin dance champion and former *Strictly* professional Karen Hardy. A Latin dance champion and former *Strictly* dancer, she lifted the trophy with

Zoe and Karen talk talent, heel-turns and tangos on the *It Takes Two* sofas.

Mark BENTON

Waterloo Road star Mark comes straight from a tour of *Hairspray*, where he dragged up to play Edna Turnblad and danced on stage every night. But the *Strictly* experience might be a little bit more comfortable.

'I wore a big fat suit, and a dress, and a big wig,' he reveals. 'When we had the heatwave in the summer it was terrible. They put a fan on you and the only bit it could get was my face! But dancing every night might help a bit when it comes to *Strictly*.'

The 47-year-old actor was born in Cleveland and joined the Middlesbrough Youth Theatre before moving on to RADA. After graduating, he got his first film role in Mike Leigh's *Career Girls* and went on to star in numerous TV series, including *Northern Lights, Early Doors* and *Land Girls.*

Mark says he decided to take up the *Strictly* offer because he fancied 'the challenge of it'.

'It's something so odd, like nothing I've ever done before,' he explains. 'I've always shied away from reality TV. I've been asked about a couple of things, but this came along and it's such an uplifting show. You're not on it just sitting in a room, you have to learn something – that was the attraction for me. Learning to dance is such a wonderful, joyful thing.'

The talented actor is delighted he will be competing alongside old friend Dave Myers. who once got him out of a sticky situation.

'We actually worked together years ago on a Catherine Cookson programme called *The Girl*,' he reveals. 'He was my stunt double! There was a scene we had to film with a big ox that was going mad and I was too scared to do it, so they dressed Dave up as me and made him do the scene instead. It's been a while since I've seen him but he is still the same lovely guy he was before.'

Apart from mastering the foxtrot and shaking his booty with his partner, Iveta Lukosiute, Mark is looking forward to sparkle and fake tan.

'That's the only reason I decided to do it really,' he laughs. 'I'm not bothered about the boogieing. Just give me the sequins! I quite fancy a leotard myself.'

Iveta
LUKOSIUTE

Iveta had a first, brief taste of *Strictly* magic when she stepped in last year to replace Aliona Vilani, who had suffered a fracture in training. She danced with presenter Johnny Ball but, sadly, the couple were first to leave.

The leggy Lithuanian says the experience was 'short but sweet ... I was disappointed for Johnny because he worked so hard and he really wanted to stay longer. But it is what it is and you can't change it. I still had a good time and I'm glad I met Johnny and his wife, who are lovely.'

Iveta started dancing aged five and began Latin training at six, winning amateur junior championships in her home country. At the age of 17, she moved to the US, where she added a love of ballroom to her passion for Latin, and six years later she went professional. She excelled in Ten Dance, a competition involving ballroom and Latin dances, and is now a two-time World Professional Champion and five-time US National Professional Champion.

After her brief appearance in the last series, Iveta joined the company for the live *Strictly* tour – and she loved every minute.

'It was amazing,' she enthuses. 'Everybody was so friendly – from the producers, to the make-up artists, professional dancers and celebrities. I had the best time of my life, on both the show and the tour.

'Knowing what to expect makes it so much easier for me and makes it even more exciting because I know how good it will be.'

When it comes to her celebrity, Iveta was looking for someone who can work and play hard – and hopes Mark will fit the bill.

'I like to dance with somebody I have a connection with because if there is chemistry, and he puts in the work, then we can really achieve something,' she says. 'I hope he will be very driven and want to do well. It's nice that he is a happy person, because it makes it so much easier if someone is having fun while they are dancing.'

The bubbly blonde was out walking in New York when she got the call to say she had been chosen for the next season – and she celebrated in suitably glamorous style.

'I was so happy I couldn't even express it,' she laughs. 'I was hoping I would be chosen for the show but once I knew for sure, I was super-excited. I went shopping, straight away. I bought some beautiful evening dresses to celebrate the good news.'

THE LIGHT FANTASTIC

'Lights, camera, action!' is the age-old cry of directors. And in the *Strictly* studio, the lights are a huge part of the magic. Not only do the spotlights follow the stars as they whirl around the floor, but the lighting department also uses video wizardry to produce an illuminated canvas, on which each couple can paint a picture with a dance. Lighting director MARK KENYON (below, right) has a team of 20 technicians and electricians working on each show, including seven in the lighting gallery and nine on the gantry – a walkway in the rafters of the studio – operating the spotlights. 'There are 12 follow spots, some of them spares,' he explains. 'As the couples stand at the top of the stairs the follow spot might be flat out, but as they walk down you have to dim the light because otherwise they burn out. As they dance, left and right across the dance floor, my colleague Darren Lovell is controlling the brightness from the gallery to prevent them being overexposed.'

Pumpkin patch. Halloween brings some new lighting challenges.

Since the 2010 redesign, lighting has come into the fore, with the video walls behind the dancers providing a backdrop and designs projected on the floors, over the arches and even on the staircase.

The genius behind the amazing graphics is David Newton, of design company Potion. Once the couples have decided on the theme for their routine, it's his job to create the appropriate setting. Even on the final day, he is tweaking the design right up to the wire.

We get a couple of days before the Friday rehearsals to make up the graphics, but it's very different seeing it on a small screen to seeing someone dancing in front of it; so things change at the last minute.

The first time we see it is on Friday and things can still change significantly. The most dramatic change we've had in rehearsals was from an Italian piazza to a secret garden, meaning different colours and a totally different look, and that has an effect on the rest of the lighting.'

David, who uses pictures, 3-D models and graphics to work his magic, says Halloween is one of the biggest challenges – especially in series 10. 'This year, we had ghost that came out of the screen for Sid Owen's *Ghostbusters* dance; so we had to use completely different technology – Electronic Video System, or EVS – but it worked really well.'

Once Potion have delivered their designs it's up to David Bishop, moving light and graphic programmer, to make it all come to life. 'Putting it all

together is a nightmare,' he admits. 'We don't see what Potion are doing until Friday, when we get 20 minutes to practise per dance. It's terrifying, but we do make it happen.'

Surrounded by a bank of ten computers during the dress run, David has to think on his feet to change colours, speeds and brightness where required. As Dani and Vincent take to the floor for the tango, the discussion turns to the red-and-black swirls on the floor. 'They're too busy,' says David. 'We need to change them.' By the live final the swirls are a less dramatic hue of purple and blue.

In front of the two Davids, a bank of screens is being carefully watched by Mark Kenyon and his team, who are controlling the brightness of the spots and the 'iris' – or light filter – on the cameras and making sure each lens matches the next.

Technicians Gemma O'Sullivan and Rachel Donaldson preside over a bewildering number of coloured knobs at the control desk and, during the show, their hands are flying up and down at impressive speed. As Mark explains, everything they do in the gallery adds to the glamour.

HD television, it's a very accurate science,' he reveals. 'About 70 per cent of it is photographic lighting, and close-ups. We major on making everybody look beautiful.'

Mark's team and Potion create an Egyptian look for Denise's final Charleston

Susanna REID

The *BBC Breakfast* presenter decided it was time to get up from her studio sofa after hearing tales from the *Strictly* dance floor.

'I've seen a lot of people do the show and many of them I've interviewed on the programme,' she explains. 'They always look like they're having a terrific, fantastic time. They talk about it as the time of their life. I fancied a bit of the fun and the sparkle myself.

'I'm not a particularly good dancer but I love dancing. There are very few things that give you that incredible rush.'

Susanna's *Breakfast* colleagues have proved a tough act to follow with two of them – Chris Hollins and Natasha Kaplinsky – taking the glitterball trophy.

'I could watch Chris Hollins and Ola Jordan's Charleston, over and over again,' she says. 'That was one of those priceless *Strictly* moments that makes you realise it is the most terrific fun. Natasha Kaplinsky was absolute perfection on the dance floor too. However, Bill Turnbull will always be my absolute hero; he was brilliant.'

The Croydon-born journalist became a regular presenter on *BBC Breakfast* in 2003 and has had numerous highlights, including interviewing the prime minister and presenting the BBC's coverage of the Oscars live from Hollywood.

In 2011, she was partnered with Robin Windsor in a *Strictly* competition for *Children in Need* against three of her fellow newsreaders, which she won. But she believes the competition will be pretty stiff in the real show.

'Sophie [Ellis-Bextor] is a phenomenal dancer,' she observes. 'Among the contestants, we've only been together a short period of time but there are some really superb dancers. I think the judges will be completely blown away.

The competition this year is really fantastic. For my part, I smile a lot apart from when the camera's on me and then I go, "Ahh!"'

Mum-of-three Susanna is partnered with new boy Kevin Clifton, and will have to face hours of training after completing her usual early-morning stint in the BBC studio. But she's refusing to be daunted by the prospect of an exhausting schedule.

She says, 'I'm just going squeeze it all in with a big smile on my face!'

Kevin CLIFTON

Last year, Kevin watched from the sidelines as his fiancée and dance partner, Karen Hauer, danced up a storm with Nicky Byrne. But helping out with the choreography and group numbers meant he was welcomed into the *Strictly* fold.

'We both said that we'd love to do it but they didn't change any of the boys, so there just wasn't a place for me,' he explains. 'But it worked out well because I could focus on supporting Karen. When it came to elimination nights, I was more stressed out than she was.

'This year it's going to be completely different. We're in competition against each other. If she shows me a move and it looks good, I'll tell her not to do it!'

As the son of former World Latin Champions Keith and Judy Clifton, Kevin started learning as a tiny tot and went on to win international open titles in 14 countries, including Italy, Germany, Spain, Japan and Singapore.

'I can't even remember my first dance steps, but I'm told I was about four,' he says. 'I've been doing it all my life.'

The hardest thing for the family was keeping Kevin's big news under wraps. But his mum and dad couldn't have been more thrilled. 'I told Mum as soon as I found out and she just went mental. She dropped the phone and then Dad had to call me back because Mum was crying – she was so excited.'

Kevin and Karen, who got engaged earlier this year, are looking forward to dancing together on the show – but Kevin says there is 'healthy competition' when it comes to lifting that glitterball.

And he admits to some nerves about the first weeks on the show. 'I'm really excited but I'm going to be nervous because it's a massive show, with millions of people watching, so a lot of pressure. Plus the professionals we're replacing are great dancers, loved by the viewers. If we're not up to their standards, there are going to be complaints. We all know that we have to do more because we have big shoes to fill – and obviously I've got to try to be better than Karen!'

A DECADE
of Dance

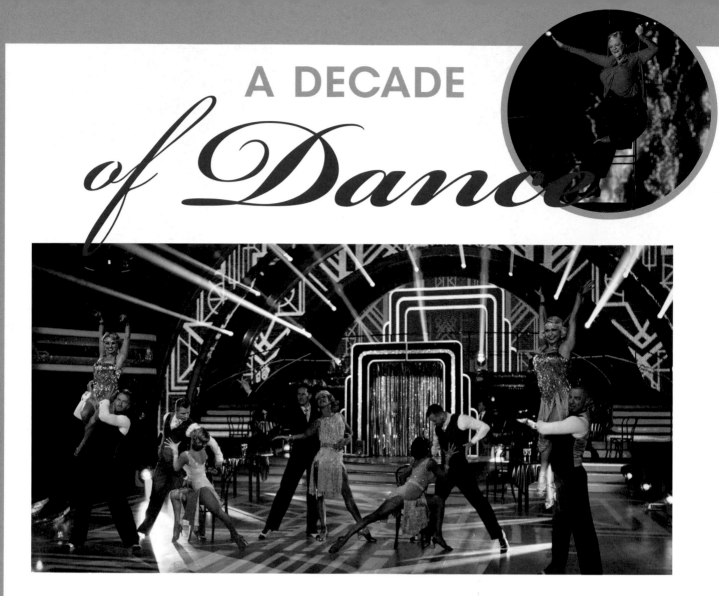

This season marks *Strictly*'s tenth year, and Saturday night just wouldn't be the same without it. In 2003, TV executive Richard Hopkins suddenly had a 'eureka' moment. 'Why not bring back *Come Dancing*,' he thought, 'but with celebrities?'

Come Dancing was one of TV's longest-running shows – airing from 1949 to 1998 – and had even featured our very own Len Goodman as both competitor and guest judge.

Richard's idea fell by the wayside until fellow executive Fenia Vardanis independently suggested *Come Dancing* should be revamped. Jane Lush, then head of BBC Entertainment, put them together, and in May 2004 *Strictly* burst on to the screen in an explosion of sequins.

Since newsreader Natasha Kaplinsky lifted that first glitterball, the competing couples have increased from 8 to 14, with only Brendan Cole and Anton Du Beke remaining from the original line-up. Seven new dances have been included and the couples have performed 1,031 dances in the main series alone, with the cha-cha-cha getting 99 outings.

'I've never forgotten Alesha Dixon's Viennese waltz,' recalls head judge Len. 'I imagined she'd be good at Latin, because she's a hot chick, but her Viennese was outstanding. Mark Ramprakash's Argentine tango and Rachel Stevens's rumba with Vincent were both absolute stonkers too.'

Other moments stand out for very different reasons. 'You forget most of the great routines but you never forget Ann Widdecombe flying on to the stage, John Sergeant's paso doble and Russell Grant being fired out of a cannon.'

STRICTLY THE BEST

Louis's win puts sports stars neck and neck with actors when it comes to winning.

3 ACTORS
Jill Halfpenny
Tom Chambers
Kara Tointon

3 SPORTS STARS
Darren Gough
Mark Ramprakash
Louis Smith

2 PRESENTERS
Natasha Kaplinsky
Chris Hollins

2 MUSICIANS
Alesha Dixon
Harry Judd

Fellow judge Craig goes back to series 2 to name one of his favourite dancers. 'I love Jill Halfpenny, because her jive was so amazing,' he says. 'But rivalling that is Denise Van Outen. Out of the boys, I love Mark Ramprakash's journey, because he came from nothing. His salsa was fabulous, even though he and Karen Hardy famously got tangled up in their microphones.'

While they might differ on the best dancer, all three male judges agree on the worst dancer ever – series 2 star Quentin Wilson. 'Without a doubt the most terrible, horrendous dancer we've had,' says Len.

With ten years on its feet, *Strictly's* popularity is still soaring, and Bruno puts that down to the programme's universal appeal.

'*Strictly* is a show that doesn't exclude anybody – young, old, male, female,' he says.

'It's the perfect shiny show for an autumn evening. It's entertaining, inspiring, fun theatre.'

Len, who filmed the pilot for the first show on his 60th birthday, says the last ten years have been a blast. 'To think that I was the first person that Bruce Forsyth turned to as a judge and said, "What do you think of that?" Those memories will live with me for ever,' he says. 'I feel so lucky. There are others from the world of ballroom who had done better as dancers, so to get picked as a judge was an honour. It's been terrific.'

The judges are now familiar faces, of course, with a huge fan base of their own. 'By now, from us, you get what you expect,' says Len. 'I'm a bit of a fuddy-duddy and moan about the lack of content or the footwork, Bruno's always on about the passion and the drama and Craig is Craig – never leaves a turn unstoned!'

Strictly QUIZ

1

Iveta Lukosiute danced with Johnny Ball in the first week of series 10. Which injured professional was she standing in for?

2

Who was runner-up in series 9, when Harry Judd lifted the glitterball?

3

Who was winner Kara Tointon's professional partner?

4

Which series 7 contestant made it to his hometown of Blackpool to dance before being eliminated?

5

Which star was shot out of a cannon in Wembley?

6

Which TV personalities are the only father and daughter who have both graced the dance floor?

7

Which screen mum got a roasting from Len over her tango, when he said, 'It was as though both legs were down one hole of your knickers.'?

8

Which formidable lady was the first eliminated in series 9?

9

Who are the only married couple to have competed in the same year?

10

Whose *Titanic* dance, with Anton, sank the judges' scores?

11

What life-changing event was on Tom Chambers' mind when he waltzed to victory in series 6?

12

Who was the first celeb to pick up a perfect score?

13

Which male singer was the celebrity guest on the 2012 Grand Final?

14

Who was guest judge in series 9, when Len had a week off?

15

Series 4 saw the introduction of two new dances – the Viennese waltz and another uplifting ballroom dance. What was it?

16

Series 3 and 4 were both won by famous players of the same sport. Which one?

17

Which children's TV character made Dani Harmer into a child star?

18

In series 7, some celebrities scored more than 40. How was this possible?

19

Which judge flew in on a broomstick during the Halloween night in series 9?

20

Who conducts the 'wonderful orchestra' introduced by Bruce each week?

WHICH JUDGE ARE YOU?

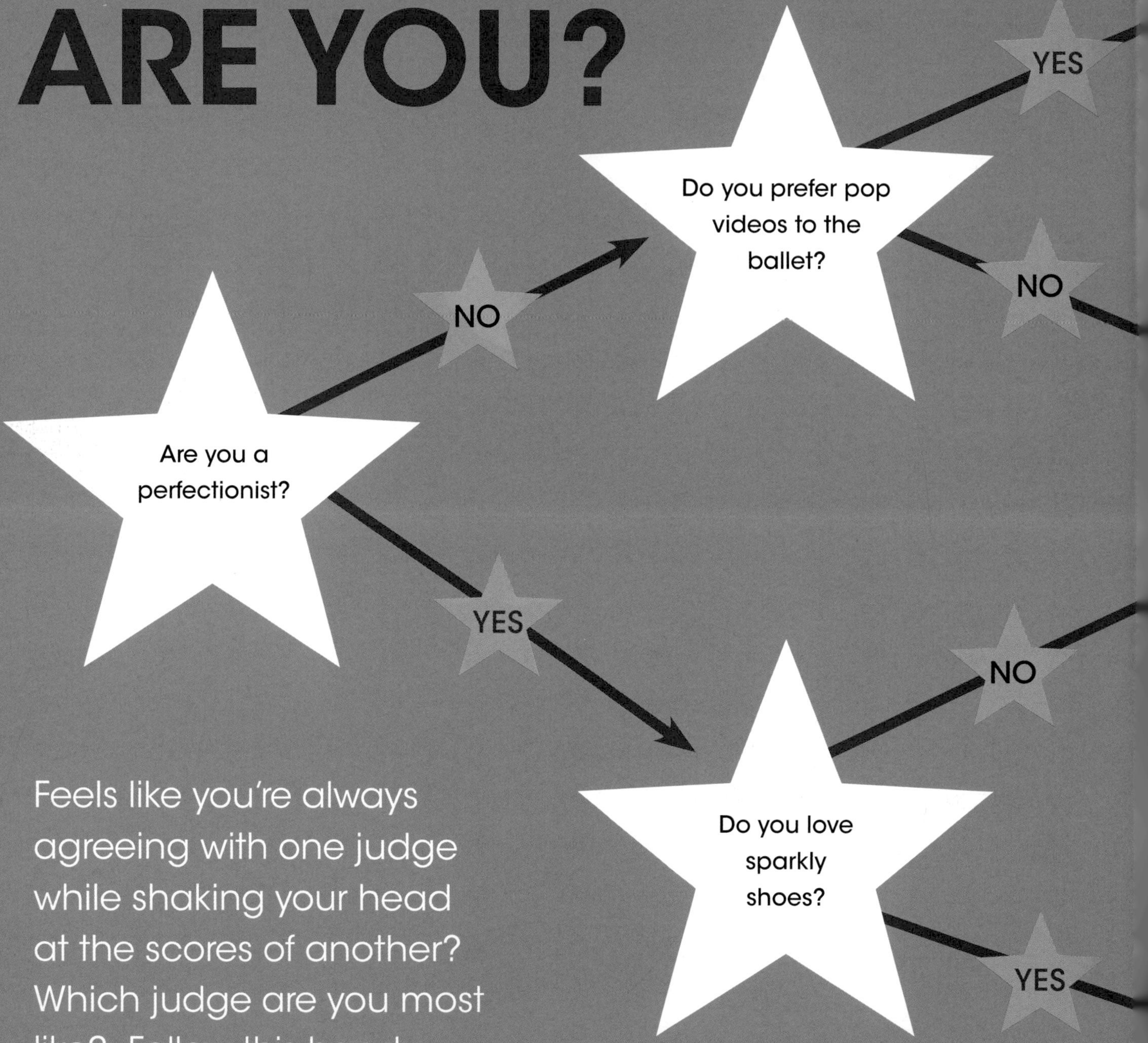

Feels like you're always agreeing with one judge while shaking your head at the scores of another? Which judge are you most like? Follow this handy flow chart to find out.

Are you a perfectionist?

NO →

Do you prefer pop videos to the ballet?

YES

NO

Do you love sparkly shoes?

NO

YES

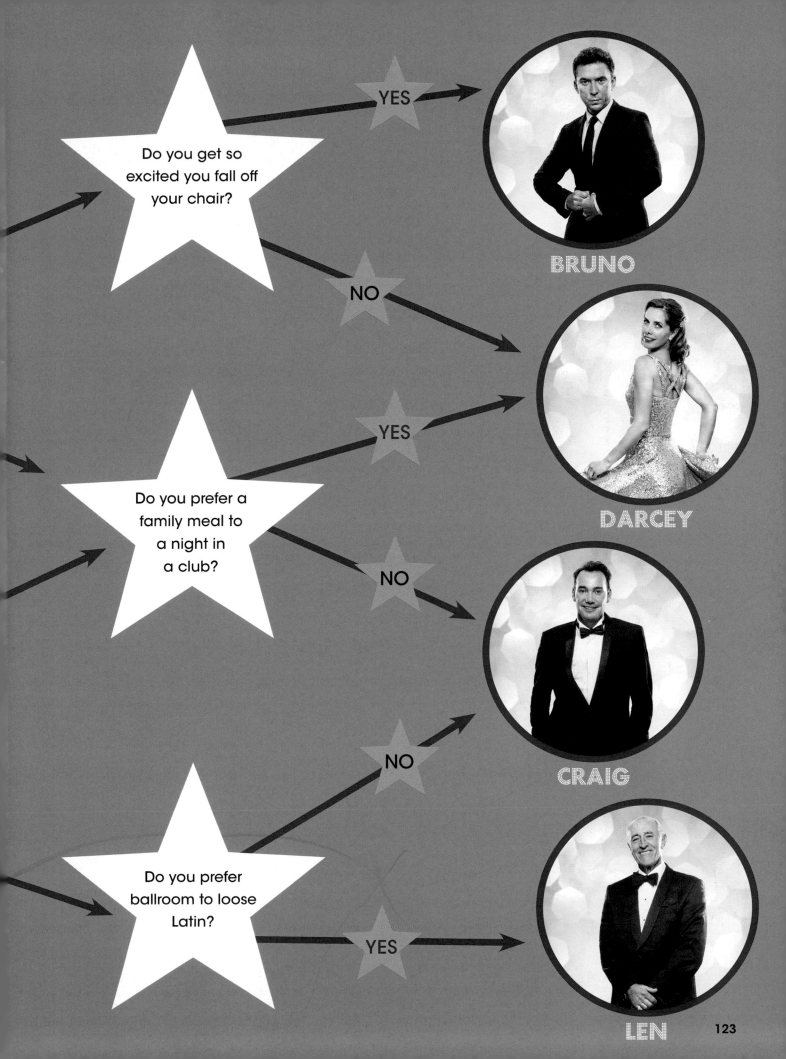

Do you get so excited you fall off your chair?

YES

BRUNO

NO

Do you prefer a family meal to a night in a club?

YES

DARCEY

NO

CRAIG

NO

Do you prefer ballroom to loose Latin?

YES

LEN

123

Week	Score	Sophie & Brendan	Patrick & Anya	Vanessa & James	Dave & Karen	Deborah & Robin	Ashley & Ola	Rachel & Pasha	Tony & Aliona
1	Yours								
	Judges'								
2	Yours								
	Judges'								
3	Yours								
	Judges'								
4	Yours								
	Judges'								
5	Yours								
	Judges'								
6	Yours								
	Judges'								
7	Yours								
	Judges'								
8	Yours								
	Judges'								
9	Yours								
	Judges'								
10	Yours								
	Judges'								
11	Yours								
	Judges'								
12	Yours								
	Judges'								
13	Yours								
	Judges'								
FINAL	Yours								
	Judges'								

JUDGE ☆

Abbey & Aljaž	Ben & Kristina	Fiona & Anton	Julien & Janette	Natalie & Artem	Mark & Iveta	Susanna & Kevin	Knocked Out
							Winner

YOU *DANCIN'?*

It's not just competing celebrities that have been inspired by *Strictly* – the show has also brought the whole nation to its feet. Thousands of people have taken up ballroom or Latin since the show began, and dance classes have been springing up all over the country.

Former *Strictly* professional **KAREN HARDY**, who runs her own dance school, says the interest in lessons stretches across all ages – and it's not just girls, either.

'It's a beautiful thing that *Strictly* has created,' she says. 'We always say that dance is for anyone from 5 to 105, but what we've noticed at our studio, and throughout England, is that boys have started coming to lessons now, as well as fathers, husbands and boyfriends. Instead of the mum at home who wants to go out for the evening to a big dance class, we're getting the whole family. That is largely thanks to

the Darren Goughs and Colin Jacksons. Recognisable sportsmen who are strong role models have said, "It's cool to dance."'

Bryan Allen, of the British Dance Council, backs up her message. 'The fantastic interest generated by *Strictly Come Dancing* has seen a considerable growth in the number of classes being offered. Some like the one-to-one instruction as shown on the programme but many prefer the group tuition, which gives a friendly and social environment.'

It is not possible to give precise figures but many thousands have been attracted to the benefits of dancing in its many forms. As Allen says, 'Dancing has three medically approved benefits. It's good for you: physically, mentally and socially.'

So if you fancy kicking up your heels but are a little nervous about starting, Karen has some sound advice. 'The first thing is to understand that everybody is nervous,' she says. 'The hardest bit is getting yourself to the studio because nerves kick in and every possible excuse will crop up. Once you take control of that and turn up, then it's up to the studio.

'Don't make excuses – get yourself to that class. Write it down, stick it on your fridge, and cancel everything to get there! If they're a good studio, and they're experienced in welcoming absolute beginners, you will never look back after taking that initial plunge.'

The former *Strictly* champ says comfortable clothing is important but that doesn't mean you can't glam up while you learn. 'We like people to feel dressed up at our studio, because we want people to feel special. But flat shoes are best, so you feel confident that you're not going to wobble. Bring along two pairs of shoes, in case one is uncomfortable.

'Don't worry about music, don't worry about steps, and don't worry that you can't do it. By the time you leave, you will have learnt the first couple of steps of two dances, sometimes three. People often walk in saying, "There's no way I can do this" and they leave saying, "Wow, I know the steps of about three dances." It's a great start.'

Opposite: Denise and James prepare to demonstrate how much can be achieved.
Below: Karen Hardy puts cricketer Mark Ramprakash through his paces.

'Don't make excuses – get yourself to that class. Write it down, stick it on your fridge, and cancel everything to get there!'

A STAGE ENTERTAINMENT AND PHIL MCINTYRE ENTERTAINMENTS IN ASSOCIATION WITH BBC WORLDWIDE PRESENTATION

BBC

Strictly Come Dancing
THE LIVE TOUR

Don't miss your chance to experience the energy and excitement of Strictly Live Tour!

17 - 19 Jan	**BIRMINGHAM** NIA	0844 338 8000
20 - 21 Jan	**LONDON** Wembley Arena	0844 815 0815
23 Jan	**LIVERPOOL** Echo Arena	0844 8000 400
24 - 26 Jan	**LEEDS** First Direct Arena	0844 248 1585
28 - 29 Jan	**SHEFFIELD** Motorpoint Arena	0114 256 56 56
30 - 31 Jan	**NEWCASTLE** Metro Radio Arena	0844 493 6666
1 - 2 Feb	**GLASGOW** The SSE Hydro	0844 395 4000
4 - 5 Feb	**NOTTINGHAM** Capital FM Arena	0843 373 3000
6 - 7 Feb	**MANCHESTER** Phones 4u Arena	0844 847 8000
8 - 9 Feb	**LONDON** The O2	08448 24 48 24

strictlycomedancinglive.com